CU00642427

In this very helpful book, R. T. Kendall challenges of all our hearts. Whatev Spirit of God can clearly spirit, rooted in self-intere is the essence of who the Pharisees were, and it was so hurtful and damaging. Ouch, sometimes on reflection, I can find that in my own heart. Thank you, R. T., for writing this convicting work that calls us all back to "being rooted and grounded in love...that you may be filled with all the fullness of God" (Eph. 3:17, 19, NKJV).

—JOHN ARNOTT
FOUNDING PASTOR, CATCH THE FIRE

I have known Dr. R. T. Kendall for many years and have a great respect for his passion for biblical truth, especially the gospel. In this crazy time of COVID-19 R. T. has developed a test with over twenty markers that identifies whether our spiritual lives have been infected with the Pharisee virus. Some may discover their case is much worse than others; some may read this on their spiritual ventilators and discover the antidote to restore their spiritual health. The other thing that is interesting is the Pharisee virus (spirit) is highly contagious. I believe you will find *You Might Be a Pharisee If...* enlightening and medicine for your soul. Enjoy a provocative, insightful, and well-written book.

—RANDY CLARK
AUTHOR, *DESTINED FOR THE CROSS*, *THERE IS MORE!*,
AND MANY BOOKS ON HEALING AND THE GIFTS OF
THE HOLY SPIRIT

Rev. Dr. R. T. Kendall, an international author, revered expositor, and generous-hearted pastor, has given us a book for self-diagnosis of the one disease we all think someone other than we ourselves have: Pharisaism. He takes our spiritual temperature, listens to our spiritual heart, checks our religious blood pressure, and lets us diagnose ourselves. With typical biblical exposition and personal application, he gives us both the diagnosis and the remedy. This is good medicine.

—JOEL C. GREGORY, PHD
PROFESSOR OF PREACHING
HOLDER OF THE GEORGE W. TRUETT ENDOWED
CHAIR IN PREACHING AND EVANGELISM,
BAYLOR UNIVERSITY

Transparent and frighteningly honest, revelation and conviction on every page, challenging and yet encouraging. The need to live for an audience of One trumpets loud and clear all through another gem of a book from R. T. Kendall. May we in this generation pursue God's honor and glory above everything else!

—GRANT BREWSTER
PASTOR, ISLAND CHURCH
BAINBRIDGE ISLAND, WASHINGTON

I was excited to read R. T.'s new book until, after I began reading it, I realized that I was the one in the crosshairs of the very point he is making! I continue to be amazed at the fact that just when I think I can see clearly enough to identify the "speck" in someone's eye, the Lord continues to remind me of the "plank" that still remains in my own eye. Thank you, R. T. Kendall, for writing another thought-provoking book!

—JEFF DOLLAR
SENIOR PASTOR, GRACE CENTER
FRANKLIN, TENNESSEE

You Might Be a Pharisee If... is not only the self-evaluation that I needed, but it's quite possibly what is needed for the church as a whole today. It pulls at the very fabric of our personal religious comforts and gets us to wrestle with the truth of performance in our pursuit of God. R. T. Kendall masterfully tears down the religious walls that are in all of us and reveals what the heart of a true believer is supposed to look like.

—CHRIS REIS
EX-NFL PLAYER, NEW ORLEANS SAINTS
NATIONAL FOOTBALL CHAMPION

Many of Jesus' most convicting words were directed at the Pharisees, yet we often avoid those parts of the Bible. Maybe we assume those harsh rebukes don't apply to us because Jesus said them to religious leaders. Yet Dr. R. T. Kendall reminds us that there is a little bit of Pharisaism in all of us. The more I read this book, the more I realized that all of Jesus' words are for me, not just the comforting messages. When you read this book, don't use it to find a speck of Pharisaism in the eyes of the people around you. Apply the message to yourself and get the log out of your own eye. I am grateful to Dr. Kendall for giving us this strong medicine.

—J. Lee Grady
Author
Director, The Mordecai Project

Dr. R. T. Kendall has long been a friend and resource to the local church. What I appreciate the most about R. T. is he loves the church enough to ask the "tough questions." I am forever indebted to him for his wisdom, insights, and friendship.

—Paul Berube
Lead Pastor, Gate City Church

The Pharisees of the worst kind flanked the ministry of Jesus everywhere He went. Every believer carries the DNA of the spirit of Pharisaism in his being and should frequently ask himself, "Might I be a Pharisee?" This book will help you honestly answer that question with lasting and helpful results.

—Jack Taylor
President, Dimensions Ministries

Contemporary Christ followers shun being labeled *a Pharisee* much like the global community in 2020 had to stay clear of those who contracted the terrible coronavirus. The World Health Organization published health and safety guidelines to protect citizens everywhere from contracting and/or spreading this highly infectious disease. In this insightful work *You Might Be a Pharisee If...*, Dr. R. T. Kendall has published health and safety guidelines to prevent our contracting the deadly disease of *self-righteousness*—the very disease Pharisees were so good at spreading. Pick up this book so you'll know how to treat the disease when you see it in others and learn how to protect yourself from getting infected.

—David D. Ireland, PhD
Senior Pastor, Christ Church
Author, *Raising a Child Who Prays* and
One in Christ

I appreciate R. T.'s book because it gets to the heart of what it means to be a Christian. R. T.'s humility, life, and ministry experience, knowledge of the Word, and deep love of God combine to provide a reliable and eminently practical guide to recognizing those telltale components in our hearts that deter us from a safe passage into His heavenly kingdom. As R. T. shows, understanding Pharisaism will refreshingly steer you clear of these obstacles. R. T. writes with truly genuine love, joy, and down-home humor that will put you at ease and lift you to ever-new places in the Lord.

—Dr. Rolland Baker
Missionary
Founder, Iris Global

R. T. Kendall's books are truly a reflection of many decades of pastoral experience, penetrating wisdom, refreshing clarity, and remarkable ability to communicate challenging theological concepts in a Bible friendly manner. R. T. Kendall is beyond question one of God's great teaching pastors and a gift to today's church. I was deeply impacted by his ministry when he spoke at Onnuri Pastor's Academy with his profound biblical insights, sensitivity to the Spirit, and passion for the gospel.

We were genuinely privileged to be in the presence of this godly servant and treasure trove of wisdom. R. T. has indeed left an indelible mark on the Onnuri Pastoral community to grow as the Lord's servants and not to remain as yesterday's men.

In *You Might Be a Pharisee If...*, R. T. exposes the attitudes, behaviors, and signs of the sin that Jesus hated the most. It shows how well-meaning Christian leaders can easily fall into the trap of legalism and self-righteousness in their ministry. Wisely, R. T. guided me to see the subtle and powerful grip of Pharisaism among so many Christian leaders including myself.

I am excited for those who will read this book reflectively and begin the process of spiritual transformation. If you want to see a revival, I recommend you get this book and read it prayerfully and allow the Holy Spirit to work in your heart so that a revival may start in your heart.

—Jae Hoon Lee
Senior Pastor, Onnuri Church
Chairman, Handong University

I've been blessed to know and learn from R. T. for almost two decades now. My life as a Jesus follower has matured in many ways as a result of the Lord using his teachings, and this book is no different. I, like R. T., grew up a Pharisee. And I, like R. T. (and most other Christians), can fall prey to the trap of being a Pharisee. I can promise, the time invested in reading this book will bring an abundant return!

—David McQueen
Lead Pastor, Beltway Park Church

You Might
Be a
Pharisee
IF...

R. T. KENDALL

You Might
Be a
Pharisee
IF...

CHARISMA
HOUSE

Visit the author's website at rtkendallministries.com.

Library of Congress Cataloging-in-Publication Data: An application to register this book for cataloging has been submitted to the Library of Congress. International Standard Book Number: 978-1-62999-878-7 E-book ISBN: 978-1-62999-879-4

Portions of this book were previously published by Charisma House as *Is Your God Too Nice?*, ISBN 978-1-62999-718-6, copyright © 2020.

21 22 23 24 25 — 9 8 7 6 5 4 3 2 1 Printed in the United States of America

To Richard and Darshika

I dedicate this book to Richard and Darshika Roe. I taught Richard the course called Evangelism Explosion. He has since led many to Christ. He later became a deacon at Westminster Chapel. Darshika was wonderfully converted at Westminster Chapel, having come from a Hindu background. I performed their marriage. I walked Darshika down the aisle as if I were her father, then walked to the platform to perform their marriage!

Table of Contents

Foreword

I F R. T. Kendall asks you to write a foreword to one of his seventy books, you feel honored. But if the foreword is for a book about Pharisees, then you start to feel shocked and maybe even self-conscious. Why not be chosen to do a foreword for R. T.'s book on "Humility" or "Wisdom" or "Sensitivity to the Spirit" and how come not "The Anointing"? Why do I get the Pharisee book? Because after reading R. T.'s insights, I had to write the foreword for this book. I've read over thirty of R. T. Kendall's books and this one is a trumpet to the church, an alarm to the pew. And now I know why I'm supposed to write this.

Who would write a book on first-century Pharisees? R. T. Kendall would because R. T. Kendall has to and the church needs him to. You may say, Tim, of all the issues, sins, and shortcomings I'm dealing with today, I'm not dealing with first-century Pharisaism. Well, you haven't read R. T. Kendall's book. And after you're done, I'm not sure you will feel the same way. I know I didn't.

My relationship with R. T. Kendall started almost twenty years ago. After reading his book on Jonah, I wrote an email inviting him to speak to our inner-city church in Detroit, and to this day I deem it as the best email I've ever written in my life. Because that email brought R. T. and Louise Kendall not just to Detroit but into Cindy's and my lives, and we've never been the same since. My crossroad moment with R. T. was at Ricky Skaggs' barbecue restaurant in Hendersonville, Tennessee. I sat there with a slab of ribs, and R. T. and I discussed theology. It was in that booth that R. T. helped me to see how secure I was in Christ as we talked about the imputed righteousness of Christ. The lights went on for me there. I believe as you read *You Might Be a Pharisee If…*the lights will go on for you.

R. T. Kendall is not just a theologian standing on his doctrinal soapbox for his colleagues to witness, but R. T. is a voice to our generation to help us to know Christ in the power of His resurrection and the fellowship of His sufferings.

*You Might Be a Pharisee If…*may be the one book of all of R. T.'s that brought me the most heart-searching. R. T. asks, "Do comments from people mean more to you than praise from God? Caution: you just might be a Pharisee." That same statement is throughout the book: "you just might be a Pharisee." And just when I thought I was out of the fray and passed one of the Pharisee tests, I was hit with another soul question— and he finished it with "you just might be a Pharisee." Then I finally yielded and screamed, "Yes, God, I am a Pharisee! Help me." Pharisees never live for an audience of one but for the crowd. That is so prevalent in my life.

I was meeting with a young pastor recently, and he asked me, "What is the greatest lesson you have learned in your almost forty years of ministry?" Without hesitation I said to him, "Proverbs 13:20: He who walks with wise men will be wise" (NKJV). The part that I knew I could do was to walk with the wise, but it would take humility and teachability to get to the second half of that verse, the "will be wise." I'm honored that R. T. would walk with me; I just pray I could return the favor by being wise like my friend. My encouragement to you is to walk with R. T. through his insight and profound challenge to the church. I guarantee you will come out wiser than when you went into this book. Walk with him through chapter four, learning how to sense sin and the conviction of the Holy Spirit again. Relive my barbecue talk with R. T. in chapter five on the righteousness that exceeds that of the Pharisees. It could be one of the most important chapters you ever read as you discover or even are reminded afresh about imputed and imparted righteousness. And finally, buckle up for the second half of the book when R. T. discusses twenty-five signs that may show you that you are a Pharisee. All I thought about as I read these twenty-five insights was Soren Kierkegaard's words "It's so much easier to become a Christian when you aren't one than to become one who you assume you already are."

R. T. Kendall's book is going to make the religious world mad. But that's OK; so did Jesus. As you read *You Might Be a Pharisee If...*, don't think of a Pharisee you could give the book to—ask the question over and over again that I did: "Is this me?"

You Might Be a Pharisee If... is a book for the church. It's a book to prepare His bride for the last great awakening on our planet before the coming of Jesus. R. T. challenges all of us to judge ourselves correctly before God does. Never has there been a more timely message than R. T. Kendall's book, *You Might Be a Pharisee If...*

—Tim Dilena
Senior Pastor, Times Square Church
New York City

Preface

AS MY BOOK *Total Forgiveness* was a spin-off from a chapter in my book *God Meant It for Good*, so the present book is a spin-off from my book *Out of Your Comfort Zone*, republished as *Is Your God Too Nice?*

This book might not have been written had not Rabbi David Rosen and I wrote our book *The Christian and the Pharisee*—his choice of title. This book was a compilation of our letters to each other in which I earnestly try to convert him (knowing, of course, that only the Holy Spirit can do this). David has remained unconvinced that Jesus of Nazareth was Israel's true Messiah. He and I have remained good friends. We correspond often, and I have managed to see him almost once a year for the last several years. I continue to pray that the Spirit of God will enlighten him. He has since been knighted by Her Majesty the Queen; he is therefore Rabbi Sir David Rosen. David has had influence with many religious leaders all over the world, including the last three popes.

In our last meeting together, in October 2019,

I pointed out how Jesus explained why the Jews rejected Him: "How can you believe, when you receive glory from one another and do not seek the glory that comes from the only God?" (John 5:44). David's response: "This does not describe all Pharisees."

In my book *Is Your God Too Nice?* I dealt with the subject of Pharisaism and in it sought to show how there is possibly a little bit of Pharisaism—as the New Testament depicts it—in all of us. The present book is an elaboration of these ideas. It is my prayer that you will be blessed by what follows.

I am grateful to Tim Dilena, the new pastor of Times Square Church of New York, for writing the foreword to this book. You might like to know that Tim is the son of the late captain Paul Dilena. As featured in both the book and the movie *The Cross and the Switchblade*, when David Wilkerson first started preaching in the streets of Brooklyn, New York, the police stopped him. But Captain Dilena overruled and said, "Let's hear what this man has to say." Captain Dilena was converted! How thrilled he would have been to know that his son is now the senior pastor of Times Square Church.

I thank Steve and Joy Strang of Charisma House for publishing this book. It is always a joy to work with the staff of Charisma. I am particularly indebted to my editor, Debbie Marrie, for her valued wisdom and help. My deepest thanks as always are to my wife, Louise—my best friend and critic.

—R. T. KENDALL
HENDERSONVILLE, TENNESSEE
SEPTEMBER 2020

Introduction

I AM A PHARISEE. "It takes one to know one," as the saying goes. I plead guilty now. I think I can also spot another Pharisee a mile away.

"It is a test of a good religion," said G. K. Chesterton, "whether you can joke about it."[1] Not that good religion is a joking matter, but whether we can laugh at ourselves and can see the good, the bad, and the ugly in the way we see ourselves. It is a test that reveals whether we will take ourselves too seriously.

My preparation for writing this book is not academic research but insight from my family and church background—which I respect to this day. If Paul the apostle could say he was brought up in a "strict manner" (Acts 22:3)—"according to the strictest party of our religion" (Acts 26:5)—I can somewhat identify with such an upbringing.

I was brought up by godly parents, even though they were legalistic. Strange as it may seem, I think one can be godly and legalistic at the same time. We were not allowed to read a Sunday newspaper, nor could we buy an ice cream cone on a Sunday. I accepted my parents' values, which were gleaned largely from strict pastors and preachers who came to our Nazarene church in Ashland, Kentucky.

My mother did not cut her hair because of Paul's reference that a woman's hair should be long (1 Cor. 11:15). She dressed modestly, making sure her sleeves went below her elbows; she did not even wear a wedding ring because of Paul's word that women should not wear gold (1 Tim. 2:9). I was not allowed to go to the movies or school dances, and the idea of wearing a class ring was out of the question. The girls in our church had the most difficult challenges; they were not allowed to wear any makeup or jewelry. I always felt sorry for them since they stood out among the students in high school.

On the other hand, my earliest memory of my father was seeing him on his knees in prayer for a half hour before he went to work. My mother would have her prayer time after my dad went to work. I can visualize her now on her knees with her hands upraised toward heaven. She always prayed with me just before I left for school.

I was saved on an Easter Sunday morning—April 5, 1942, aged six, at my parents' bedside. I had been crying and said to my parents I wanted to be saved; I felt I needed to confess my sins. My father had the perspicuity to say, "We don't need to wait until we get to church; we can pray now." The only sin I can recall was rudely talking back to my parents. But I got up from my knees with assurance that my sins were forgiven. I remember it as though it were yesterday.

My church was noisy—people called us "Noisyrenes"—not so much from the singing but the shouting of praises to God. It was common to see men and women walking up and down the aisles of the church waving handkerchiefs with tears rolling down their faces. Whatever one might say of such emotionalism, I can also say there was something in the atmosphere that made me want to be saved at the age of six.

As I grew older, I often felt out of place before the other students and neighborhood friends. They knew I could not go to movies or dances and it was indeed embarrassing. They knew also I went to the noisy Church of the Nazarene on 22nd and Bath Avenue, but I myself for some reason never entered into the shouting. But it did not stop people from jeering at me, "R. T.'s a Nazarene, R. T.'s a Nazarene."

The Church of the Nazarene has been known for its stress on holiness. In the old days they stressed that there were two works of grace—being saved and sanctified. The latter was also called the baptism of the Holy Spirit, although such was never in their thinking connected to speaking in tongues. We were taught that you could live above sin. If you sinned, you lost your salvation. The idea of eternal security or predestination was not even remotely a part of their teaching.

Nazarenes today are not what they used to be. They

are quieter, more middle class, and are divided about whether sanctification is a conscious instantaneous work of grace or a process. I still love them and am in touch with them. My old alma mater—Trevecca Nazarene University in Nashville—kindly gave me a doctor of divinity degree a few years back.

These things said, although I have been led away from the legalism and some of the doctrines of my former church, such preparation probably explains why to this day I have been able to shrug off criticisms of my faith and theology. I grew up accepting a stigma. I can never forget too that I was saved in that denomination. As a teenager I read my Bible faithfully and managed to pray for fifteen minutes every day before I went to school. I have had a strong prayer life ever since, and I am thankful to God for my background—despite its oddities.

Dr. Martyn Lloyd-Jones (1899–1981) used to say to me again and again, "Don't forget your Nazarene background. It is what has saved you." By *saved* he meant being spared of the coldness and deadness of so many of the reformed ministers who were around. "Perfectly orthodox and perfectly useless" is the way he described some of them. It is why he put me in Westminster Chapel.

One might understandably refer to the strictness of my background as Pharisaism, which I will elaborate on in the pages of this book. I do know I have often sympathized with modern Jews praying at the Western Wall in Jerusalem. I have been present on some Fridays near sundown when the praying and the crying out to *Adonai*—which means Lord—truly sounded like "Noisyrenes."

Several years ago I became a part of the Alexandria Peace Process in Israel. It was led by the Archbishop of Canterbury and his envoy Canon Andrew White. The purpose was to see if religious leaders of various points of view could bring peace to the Middle East. It was through this that I met Rabbi Sir David Rosen and the late president of the Palestinians, Yasser Arafat.

I was also given a surprising introduction to modern-day Pharisaism.

Part I:

Introducing the Pharisees and Pharisaism

CHAPTER 1

What Is a Pharisee?

*But woe to you, scribes and
Pharisees, hypocrites!*

—MATTHEW 23:13

I N THE EARLY days when I was a part of the Alexandria Peace Process, I was invited to a *Shabbat* (Sabbath) meal on a Friday evening. It was held in the kosher Mount Zion Hotel in Jerusalem. I have since stayed there many times. The *Shabbat* meal was arranged and carried out by Rabbi Sir David Rosen, this being the first time I met him. As he explained what was happening during our meal, I was perplexed over how he was so complimentary of a Pharisee. It seemed that David was even professing to *be* a Pharisee. I was very surprised.

When it became appropriate to ask questions, I asked: "Rabbi Rosen, if I have understood you this evening, you are actually speaking of a Pharisee in a most complimentary manner; you have even given the impression that you call yourself a Pharisee. Have I got this right?"

He replied: "Absolutely. The New Testament doesn't give the Pharisees a good press." He therefore made it clear that he is unashamedly a Pharisee, but not like those described in the New Testament. He wears the label Pharisee as a badge of honor.

This meant I have much to take in and a lot to learn. For one thing, David Rosen does not fit the caricature of the Pharisee as described in the New Testament. So in the present book—*You Might Be a Pharisee If...*—I do not have someone like David in mind. For one thing, he is too British to be much like the Pharisees portrayed in the New Testament! I will say, however, that in our book *The Christian and the Pharisee*, I did conclude that—at the end of the day—David was every bit a Pharisee in the issue that ultimately mattered: he made void the Word of God by tradition (Mark 7:13). He did not support his defense with Scripture but by the commentaries of the rabbis.

That said, I believe that the Pharisees described in the New Testament were what Jesus said they were: "Everything they do is done for people to see: They make their phylacteries wide and the tassels on their garments long" (Matt. 23:5, NIV).

Pharisaism is the belief and practice of an ancient

Jewish sect called Pharisees. They apparently emerged in the second century BC and thrived during the time of Jesus. They were a strict sect made up mostly of ordinary Jews, unlike the Sadducees, who were members of the families of priests. The Pharisees were far more numerous than the Sadducees but not as prestigious.

The Pharisees kept closely to the Mosaic Law. They often embellished the Law with countless rules so that these rules were very hard to keep. They saw themselves as a cut above everybody else. They counted work on the Sabbath as walking more than a kilometer from one's town, carrying any kind of load, or lighting a fire in their home. It led to people being concerned to keep the law in every detail. The Pharisees believed that their rules built a fence around the Law so that by keeping these rules people would be in less danger of disobeying the actual Law of God.

The Aramaic word for *Pharisee* means separatism or one who is separated. Pharisees were known for their adherence to tradition, especially strictness of religious observance, as we will see later. Whether the Pharisees got "good press" comes down to whether Jesus' words are reliable. If they are reliable, as I believe they are, the popular perception of Pharisaism being the essence of self-righteousness is fair and just. Jesus also used the term *hypocrites* interchangeably with the Pharisees. This does not mean that all Pharisees were hypocrites, but, generally speaking, most of them were or Jesus would not have described them as He did.

In the four Gospels, Pharisees are portrayed almost entirely as bad guys. And yet on one occasion Jesus accepted an invitation to have dinner with a Pharisee (Luke 11:37). The meal was paralleled by Jesus exposing the hearts of the Pharisees—whom He tended to put together in one lump. The Pharisee was astonished to see that Jesus did not first wash before dinner. Jesus, however, knew exactly what this Pharisee was thinking—and called Pharisees "fools."

> Now you Pharisees cleanse the outside of the cup and of the dish, but inside you are full of greed and wickedness. You fools!
> —Luke 11:39–40

The *Free Dictionary* defines Pharisaism as "(1) the doctrines and practices of Pharisees and (2) hypocritical observance of the letter of religious or moral law without regard for the spirit; sanctimoniousness."[1] It goes on to say that Pharisaism is "the behavior of a sanctimonious and self-righteous person." One definition of *sanctimonious* is making a show of being morally superior to other people. It can also refer to making your face indicate (sometimes with a frown or even tears showing grave concern) how moral, godly, or holy you think you are—or what you want others to *think* you are. Pharisees were experts at this. It would seem therefore that there is a universal perception that Pharisees were a self-righteous lot.

We are all born Pharisees! We are all—without exception—born with a deadly predisposition to self-righteousness. It is the essence of original sin. Another way of putting it is that self-righteousness is essentially defensiveness. That is what you see in the original sin of Adam and Eve: defensiveness. After Adam and Eve sinned in the Garden of Eden, their self-righteousness and defensiveness surfaced quickly. Neither blamed themselves. Neither said, "I have sinned; I am so sorry." The opposite was true.

Adam blamed Eve. "The woman whom you gave to be with me—she gave me fruit of the tree, and I ate" (Gen. 3:12). One might even infer that Adam was blaming God; he was virtually saying, "The woman *You* gave to be with me made me do it—it is Your fault because You gave her to me."

Eve then blamed the serpent who had tempted her. "The serpent deceived me, and I ate" (v. 13). We don't need to be taught Pharisaism; it is as natural as eating apple pie. This is the way we are all born. To quote St. Augustine (354–430), humankind should be seen in four stages:

1. Man was born *posse peccare*—able to sin

2. Man after the fall was *non posse non peccare*—not able not to sin

3. Man after regeneration (born again) is *posse non peccare*—able not to sin

4. Man after glorification in heaven will be *non posse peccare*—unable to sin

We are all born as Adam was *after* the fall. No person since Adam's fall in Eden was born as Adam was originally created—without sin. Pelagius (360–420), Augustine's fierce opponent, took the heretical view—that we are born sinless as Adam was originally created. The Bible says the opposite: "Behold, I was brought forth in iniquity, and in sin did my mother conceive me" (Ps. 51:5). We all "go astray from birth, speaking lies" (Ps. 58:3). This is why it is written,

> None is righteous, no, not one; no one under-
> stands, no one seeks for God. All have turned
> aside, together they have become worthless; no
> one does good, not even one. Their throat is an
> open grave, they use their tongues to deceive.
> The venom of asps is under their lips. Their
> mouth is full of curses and bitterness. Their
> feet are swift to shed blood; in their paths are
> ruin and misery, and the way of peace they
> have not known. There is no fear of God before
> their eyes.
>
> —ROMANS 3:10–18

In a word: "All have sinned and fall short of the glory of God" (Rom. 3:23). We are not sinners merely because we sin; we sin because we are born sinners. The essence of sin is self-righteousness.

The issue, therefore, is not how to become a Pharisee but how to be rid of Pharisaism! The question is: Can we be completely rid of Pharisaism? Paul said that "where the Spirit of the Lord is, there is freedom" (2 Cor. 3:17). That is why the more we are filled with the Spirit, the less defensive we are. The greatest freedom is having nothing to prove.

I wrote the book *Jealousy: The Sin Nobody Talks About*. Some of my friends tell me it is my best book! I wrote a sequel to it—originally called *Self-Righteousness: The Sin Nobody Admits To*. My publisher talked me out of this title (they said it wouldn't sell well) and called it *The Power of Humility*. It is the exact same book—not one sentence changed. I so wanted it to be called *Self-Righteousness: The Sin Nobody Admits To*. Be that as it may, the present book is intended to be an exposure of our self-righteousness. I pray we all can read it and enjoy it and, hopefully, laugh at ourselves. And yet it is not a joking matter.

CHAPTER 2

The Sin Jesus Hated the Most

*The Pharisee stood by himself and prayed: "God, I
thank you that I am not like other people."*

—LUKE 18:11, NIV

THE QUOTE ABOVE is taken from the teaching of Jesus. It comes from a parable—a form of communication Jesus used all the time. When I read this particular parable about the Pharisee and the tax collector, I laugh. "God, I thank you that I am not like other people." Was Jesus laughing when He told this parable? Did those who heard it laugh?

What is funny to me might not be funny to you. One's sense of humor is almost certainly pertaining to one's personality, upbringing, or even mood at the time. Furthermore, culture plays a big part. What may be funny in Spain may not be funny in Germany. I know for certain that what is funny in England is often not funny at all in America. British comedians seldom are seen as hilarious in America as they are in England. The British have a subtle sense of humor; Americans often don't get British jokes at all. In Ireland they have jokes about the English. In England they have French jokes. In Poland they have Russian jokes. In southern Indiana they have Kentucky jokes.

There is "a time to laugh" (Eccles. 3:4). Does this mean God has a sense of humor? I would say yes. After all, we are made in the image of God (Gen. 1:27). Otherwise why do we laugh? A merry or joyful heart does good like medicine (Prov. 17:22). I find laughing emancipating, especially if I have not had a good laugh for a while.

So was Jesus laughing at Pharisees generally when He told the parable focusing on the words, "God, I thank you that I am not like other people," making fun of the Pharisees' lack of objectivity about themselves? Possibly. Was He smiling? Possibly. Was He weeping with concern that people could be so self-righteous? That is also possible, especially if one thinks Jesus never laughed or had no sense of humor. When Jesus said that hypocrites sound a trumpet to call attention to their giving to the poor, was He making fun of them? Surely He was!

Is it not funny that Jesus said you have a log in

your eye when you see a speck in another's eye? That surely must have made His immediate hearers laugh. Or when Jesus said that it is easier for a rich man to enter the kingdom than it is for a camel to go through an eye of a needle—whatever that was (Matt. 19:24). Some probably laughed when Jesus called Herod a fox (Luke 13:32). When we get to heaven and see a video replay of Jesus' referring to Pharisees as He did, I predict we will see that the common people—who heard him gladly (Mark 12:37, KJV)—often laughed their heads off at the way Jesus poked fun at the Pharisees. The Pharisees were not popular with the populace.

I think, therefore, that people laugh at us when we are self-righteous like the Pharisees. Do you enjoy being laughed at? Caution: people may be laughing at you owing to your being so much like a Pharisee. Your sanctimoniousness might impress some, but probably not one who severely differs with you—if you are a politician and they are taking the opposite side of your view. Oh yes, politicians—not just preachers—can sound *so* sanctimonious when upholding what they think will impress voters. You may easily see their hypocrisy as they speak.

It is hard not to laugh at some Christians—for example, melancholy Christians who moralize you for the way you dress and then look like they just fell off a covered wagon! Or do you look at them with pity, seeing they are so blind to the way they appear to the world?

Therefore being like a Pharisee is a no-joke thing. It is awful. God hates it. Jesus hated it. It quenches and grieves the Holy Spirit. It hurts the testimony of the church. And yet we can *only* see it in ourselves by the gracious work of the Holy Spirit. "Modesty is my greatest quality," said comedian Jack Benny. He was joking of course. But some people actually believe this about themselves. The Pharisees actually believed they were righteous before God because of their outward good works.

Indeed, whether actual Pharisees or not, anyone depending on his or her personal righteousness to save himself or herself will cause the person to forfeit salvation in Jesus Christ. Paul, himself a Jew and brought up as a Pharisee, said,

> Brothers, my heart's desire and prayer to God for them [Jews generally] is that they may be saved. For I bear them witness that they have a zeal for God, but not according to knowledge. For, being ignorant of the righteousness of God, and seeking to establish their own, they did not submit to God's righteousness. For Christ is the end of the law for righteousness to everyone who believes.
> —Romans 10:1–4

I have often asked non-Christians, "If you were to stand before God and He were to ask you, 'Why should I let you into My heaven?'" I invariably receive a reply that reflects their own self-righteousness. Even an atheist will say this.

For example, during the last twenty years I was at Westminster Chapel, I spent two hours every Saturday working with a street evangelism team we called the Pilot Lights. We gave out Christian pamphlets in Victoria, around Big Ben, and in Buckingham Gate. When a person would say, "But I don't believe in heaven, I don't believe in God," I would say: "But if there really was a heaven and you did stand before God and He asked you, 'Why should I let you into My heaven,' what would you then say?"

The reply almost invariably was something like this: "I have been good to people. I have been kind. I have lived a good life. I haven't done anything terribly wrong." In other words, *all* people reveal that they are—at bottom—self-righteous. This is because we are products of the fall; we are born *non posse non peccare*—not able not to sin.

In other words, when I say I am good enough to get to heaven by my good works, I sin right then! To say that or even to *think* that is to sin. Only the Holy Spirit enables one to see this for herself or himself.

One must not forget that many of the Pharisees in Jesus' day were in some sense pious men. Some scholars reckon that when Jesus described the Pharisee in the parable in Luke 18:9–14, some Pharisees really did such things as he boasted of—fasting twice a week and giving a tenth of all they earned, not to mention the fact that they would never be guilty of wrongdoing such as robbing someone or physically committing adultery. They were regarded as the truly righteous people of their day. They were without question the backbone of their synagogues and would in some cases be like certain evangelical Christians today who carry their big black Bibles to church and would never smoke or drink a drop of alcohol or watch a movie that was anything but for the whole family. But they tended to look down on those who did not keep their rules and called such people "sinners."

Never forget too that Nicodemus the Pharisee was a secret follower of Jesus. He was also converted (John 19:39). The apostle Paul was a Pharisee before he was converted. Therefore, if you know self-righteous people who seem a million miles away from the kingdom, remember that God can save Pharisees.

When I first came across John Newton's (1725–1807) hymn "In Evil Long I Took Delight," my heart was set ablaze because I considered how self-righteous I have been. Whereas Newton probably referred to his wicked past in terms of being so promiscuous before he was converted, my past was the opposite. Whereas John Newton's "wild career" was debauchery, my wild career was feeling so righteous. I honestly came to see that my righteousness was as evil in God's sight as Newton's sinful past was.

What had happened to me—I am ashamed to say—was that I began to be so self-righteous owing to my having departed from my old background, forfeiting my family's approval and striking out alone. I became smug and very pleased with myself. I needed a wake-up call. God was gracious to me. Here are the words of this wonderful hymn.

> In evil long I took delight,
> Unawed by shame or fear,
> Till a new object struck my sight,
> And stopp'd my wild career.
> I saw one hanging on a tree,
> In agonies and blood,
> Who fix'd His languid eyes on me,
> As near His cross I stood.
> Sure, never to my latest breath
> Can I forget that look:
> It seem'd to charge me with His death,
> Though not a word He spoke.
> My conscience felt and own'd the guilt,
> And plunged me in despair:
> I saw my sins His blood had spilt,
> And helped to nail Him there.
> A second look He gave which said,
> "I freely all forgive:
> This blood is for thy ransom paid:

> I die, that thou mayest live."
> Thus while His death my sin displays
> In all its blackest hue,
> Such is the mystery of grace,
> It seals my pardon too.[1]

I therefore take the view that one should consider how our self-righteousness is as evil in God's sight as the grossest sin may be in ours.

Here is (to me) a funny story. It comes from Dr. Martyn Lloyd-Jones, who relished telling this story. He told it to me twice, and it was funnier the second time. It is in another book I wrote, but too good not to mention here. It is about two unforgettable weeks that he and Mrs. Lloyd-Jones spent on holiday in America a good number of years ago: one week in West Virginia, the other in Michigan. The first week was with a very religious couple at a resort in White Sulphur Springs, West Virginia. They had all their meals together, but this couple, according to Dr. Lloyd-Jones, could not finish a meal without speaking negatively about "these so-called Christians who smoke and drink."

For one thing, said the man, it is "blowing away money," wasting God's provision. Dr. Lloyd-Jones said that they merely listened without expressing an opinion, but decided to ask the lady, who dressed very fashionably, how much her dress cost. Things got very quiet as it was ridiculously expensive. When the week was over, although they enjoyed much of it,

Dr. Lloyd-Jones told me that both he and Mrs. Lloyd-Jones were glad the week was over and were relieved that they didn't have to listen anymore about "these so-called Christians who smoke and drink."

But there is more. One more week to go. Their next stop was in Grand Rapids, Michigan, where they were to spend a week. The man who came to pick them up at the airport was smoking a big cigar. They were immediately amused at the contrast between the previous week and what would apparently be coming. So when they arrived at their new host's home he said, "Doctor, would you like a whiskey?" Dr. and Mrs. Lloyd-Jones were intrigued at the difference in Christians in America. He was convinced that both couples—in West Virginia and Michigan—were good Christians.

And yet the story continues. On the Sunday night after the church service in which Dr. Lloyd-Jones preached, he noticed a Howard Johnson's restaurant in Grand Rapids as they drove. "Oh look," said the doctor, "there's a Howard Johnson's restaurant. I love their ice cream. Do you suppose we could stop and have some?" Things went quiet, but the host politely pulled over and went into the parking lot. As they sat at the table, Dr. Lloyd-Jones noticed that his hosts were quiet, so he spoke up: "Is anything wrong?"

"No, of course not," the man replied.

"Now look here," said Dr. Lloyd-Jones, "we have

been together for a few days and something is clearly wrong. Please tell me what it is."

The man finally agreed. "The problem is that today is the Sabbath and we do not buy anything on the Sabbath."

Dr. Lloyd-Jones added that when he and Mrs. Lloyd-Jones went to their room, he said to her, "It seems that everybody has to have something they are against, so they feel a bit righteous. I wonder what it is with us; there must be something!"

Whatever the case, this is true with so many of us; it seems that there are one or two areas, at least, in which we have strong views about something. These views may unconsciously make us think they compensate for other liberties we allow for ourselves (if not too many know about them!). This reminds me of a joke I've heard that asks what the difference is between Baptists and Episcopalians. The answer is that the Episcopalians speak to each other in the wine store. I hope that doesn't offend any readers. It's a humorous way to illustrate what I have seen a thousand times: the best of people have their secret sins—even if they are not sins but controversial practices they allow. Equally they have one or two strong views about this or that, which gives them a feeling they haven't gone completely off the deep end.

I am also reminded of the story of when the great Charles Spurgeon (1834–1892), who loved a cigar, met the famous D. L. Moody (1837–1899). Moody rebuked Spurgeon for smoking. Spurgeon replied that there was not one word in the Bible about "this," referring to his cigar, but that there was a lot in the Bible about "that," gently poking Moody's extended stomach.

As for "rules," I am often asked by my British friends, "Why do preachers in America never seem to say a word against being fat and overweight?" This was always an awkward question put to me, especially knowing I had many precious friends who were overweight. Moreover, these are people who sincerely love the Lord. This kind of question would come up nearly every time we would have an American choir come to Westminster Chapel to sing. I was always sadly conscious, seeing huge, overweight people make their way to the gallery on each side of the pipe organ to sing for us. As I listened—and watched—I knew exactly what my people were thinking.

I did indeed wonder if pastors in the United States ever touched on the matter of our bodies being temples of the Holy Spirit when it comes to food. So, after our retirement in America, imagine my amazement when I slipped into a church one Sunday morning to hear a sermon titled "Fat Christians." I thought, "Oh good. What courage this pastor has. I never thought I would see the day a minister would address this matter." But the sermon was rebuking Christians who were fat in Bible knowledge and never witnessed to the lost.

Living in America again, I do sympathize with people who are overweight. They do not want to be this way. And yet I think of the way food is pushed at us morning, noon, and night, and how sugar is added to cereal, ketchup, and many other things; hidden fat in so much food—not to mention the inexpensive restaurants that often include "all you can eat" buffets. I've come to realize that Christians who do not smoke or drink often tend to compensate with food.

These lines may put some readers out of their comfort zone. I don't mean to be unfair. But I would say lovingly that our bodies are temples of the Holy Spirit (1 Cor. 6:19–20; 2 Cor. 6:16). It is now well known that smoking causes cancer. But according to the Harvard School of Public Health, obesity is linked to as many as eleven types of cancer.[2] This is to say nothing of diabetes, heart problems, high blood pressure, kidney disease, and a multitude of other ailments.

As for witnessing to the lost, our appearance can speak more loudly than words, and I often wonder what non-Christians must think about us who lack self-discipline in our private lives. However, the problem is that issues such as smoking and drinking become like the Pharisees' rules which you had to keep or be looked down on.

Given the fact that Pharisees were pious, faithful, and the stalwarts of the synagogues in ancient Judaism, why was Jesus so hard on them? Should He not have congratulated them, as if to say, "You are greatly needed here in Jerusalem these days. I can't imagine what things would be like were it not for you." No. He never congratulated them once or gave the slightest hint that they were either needed or appreciated. He was harsh and rugged with them. Why? The answer to this question, which will come clearer as we proceed, is why the present chapter is so important to this book.

What is most interesting to me is that Jesus was patient, loving, and gracious to the woman caught in the sin of adultery, unlike the Pharisees who were delighted and supposedly indignant that they found this woman in the act of sin (John 8:3–11). Jesus never appeared to show tender feelings toward the Pharisees. He was not nice to them, despite the fact that they upheld the infallibility of the Bible, believed in resurrected life beyond the grave (unlike the Sadducees), and adhered to a number of practices that Jesus also affirmed.

When I was a young Christian, I used to wonder why so much attention was given in the four Gospels to the Pharisees since they do not exist today. Was this not a waste of space? Why should we have to read about irrelevant people? I have since learned, of course, that Pharisees do exist today. And I fear I am one of them—in too many ways! But the other reasons we must listen to what Jesus said to them and about them include the following:

- His words were infallible.

- His judgment perfectly mirrored the will of the Father (John 5:19).

- We too would be the objects of Jesus' firm words to the degree we also are Pharisees.

We are not exempt. His ruthless exposure of the ways of the Pharisees bears our attention. If Jesus was angry with them then, the Father feels the same way about us now.

What Jesus, therefore, said to the Pharisees—and about them—must be taken seriously and applied to our lives today. I for one do not want to be a Pharisee. Do you think there is a possibility you could be a Pharisee? To the degree I am one I should be most uncomfortable. If Jesus was not nice to the ancient Pharisees, I should be very worried indeed that He will not be nice to me if I am very like them.

CHAPTER 3

The Pharisees' Comfort Zone

*They loved the glory that comes from man more than
the glory that comes from God.*

—JOHN 12:43

WHEN LOUISE AND I lived in Fort Lauderdale, we came across friends who had a Scofield Bible. I had heard of it, but never saw one. I was puzzled when they would quote from it, claiming they were quoting the Word of God. I knew the Bible fairly well and said, "That's not in the Bible." "Oh yes it is, here it is." Then they handed me their Bible, and I noticed immediately that it was *not* Scripture they were quoting at all! These people were not able to see the difference between Holy Scripture and the comments that Dr. Scofield had put in the margin, as we will see further below.

It might interest you to know that the Scofield Bible is to this day the best-selling book published by Oxford University Press. OUP was given the rights nearly a hundred years ago and it has helped pay their expenses over the years more than any other publication. One of the reasons that premillennialism (the belief that Christ will return before the thousand-year reign in Revelation 20) is so popular in America is that so many have followed the Scofield Bible all their lives. I am not saying that those who follow this Bible are Pharisees; I am only pointing out how easy it is for some to assume that Dr. Scofield's comments are the same as Holy Scripture.

The Tradition of the Pharisees

The extra-biblical rules of the Pharisees started as traditions and turned into requirements to prove you loved God and respected the Law. Some Pharisees came up to Galilee all the way from Jerusalem just to ask Jesus, "Why do your disciples break the tradition of the elders? For they do not wash their hands when they eat!" (Matt. 15:1–2). Imagine being so threatened by Jesus that one walks for three days just to see why He did not keep certain rules. This washing of hands was not merely a health matter, by the way; it was a ritualistic action that showed you adhered to the "party line."

Is tradition important to you? Tradition was very important to the Pharisees. This doesn't make you a Pharisee. There is nothing particularly wrong with tradition. Sometimes it is quite valuable. The problem is, we end up equating it with the Word of God and, if we are not careful, find it difficult to separate the two, thus making tradition idolatrous.

As I said, some good people do this with a Scofield Bible. This popular Bible has notes that accompany the Word of God that have unwittingly led many Christians, perhaps more so in America, not to know the difference between Scofield's own comments (some of which are good) and the unedited Word (which alone is infallible). I have had people headedly quote "scripture" to me from a Scofield Bible only to discover they were reading what Scofield said in the margins or at the bottom of each page.

My point is this: When Scriptures and commentaries on Scriptures are put alongside each other with equal authority so that one is revered as much as the other, it is idolatry. That is what the Pharisees did with their rules that turned into traditions and then turned into Law.

I used to say that England is the most traditional country in the world, and Westminster Chapel was the most traditional church in England. Sandy Millar lovingly said to me that we were "back in the '60s," meaning that our style at Westminster Chapel resonated with the way churches were in the 1960s. I took him seriously, tried to make some changes, and was grateful for a friend who would speak like that to me. And this was near the end of my time there! For I too am comfortable with leaving things be lest we rock the boat and cause trouble.

How They Found Significance

Any psychologist, including a Christian psychologist, will tell you that we were made to feel significant. Dale Carnegie (1888–1955), author of *How to Win Friends and Influence People*, says that the strongest urge in the human race is to feel important. We were made this way. A person who does not find significance will end up with all sorts of problems, including severe emotional problems.

The question is: How do we feel significant? The answer is: in God. If we don't find our significance in God, mainly in His Son Jesus Christ, we will be pursuing unjust goals—the problem with God's ancient people. "I was enraged by their *sinful greed*" (Isa. 57:17, NIV, emphasis added). The phrase *sinful greed* comes from a Hebrew word that essentially means unjust gain.[1]

And that was much of the reason for the Pharisees' problem. Mind you, they did not think there was a problem in the first place. But there were very serious problems indeed. And one of them was that they sought to achieve significance in being admired. "They love to be greeted with respect in the market-places and to be called 'Rabbi' by others" (Matt. 23:7, NIV). "They loved human praise more than praise from God" (John 12:43, NIV). This was the essence of their comfort zone: being applauded, being complimented, being respected, and being openly referred to. Do this, and you had no problem with them. Jesus didn't, and He had problems with them. These pious men were right in the middle of the conspiracy to have Jesus crucified (John 11:45–51).

Is it not amazing to discover how some people who on the surface seem so godly can become so mean when we cross them? Religious people are the meanest people in the world. Let them remain undisturbed in their comfort zones and they are as sweet as the god-father of the Mafia with his grandchildren. But cross them? Oh dear.

They further sought significance like this: they compared themselves with others—always people they could safely label sinners. That way they always came out on top. So in the aforementioned parable, the Pharisee boasted of his good works, then added: "God, I thank you that I am not like other people—robbers, evil doers, adulterers—or even like this tax collector" (Luke 18:11, NIV). We can all find someone less righteous to whom we can compare ourselves and, therefore, come out smelling like rose. It's been said that "comparisons are odious," referring to comparisons of one person against another; yet it is perhaps even more odious when we do this to make ourselves look good—"At least I'm not as bad as so-and-so."

The Pharisees even did this when it came to the sainted dead. They piously lamented that the great men of God of the past—prophets, for example—were not appreciated in their own day; some were even persecuted. They would lead the way in extolling the virtues of these great people of yore and proved it by building tombs for them and decorating their graves. Who else was doing this? No one. "No one else cares," said the Pharisees. "But we do. We will even have annual conferences and intelligent lectures that show today's generation what ought to be happening." Moreover, "If we had lived in the days of our ancestors, we would not have taken part with them in shedding the blood of the prophets" (Matt. 23:30, NIV). They believed they were not only a cut above the professing believers of their day but also better than anyone else in previous generations. In this way they found significance.

They also got their sense of significance in the way they dressed. Said Jesus, "Everything they do is done for people to see: They make their phylacteries wide and the tassels on their garments long" (Matt. 23:5,

NIV). Dress is very important to a Pharisee; always has been, always will be. They will not be the slightest bit convicted over holding a grudge or speaking evil of fellow believers, but they go to great pains to look good. They want to look more than nice, so people will say, "I love that suit. I love that dress. I love your hair."

Do comments from people mean more to you than praise from God? Caution: you just might be a Pharisee.

Louise and I will never forget attending a large Christian convention in Dallas many years ago. At the time, both of us had become very "proper" Brits and were not prepared for the advice a dear American friend gave Louise: "Bring at least two sets of clothes for each day. And you might want to bring different colors of nail polish to go with the various outfits. Most of the women take that little bit of extra time to coordinate their colors that way."

I remember another example of this. At a camp meeting, the district superintendent of my old denomination was one of two preachers, and the other was a Scottish preacher who had deeply impacted me. The Scot reportedly came to that camp meeting to preach with ten sermons and one suit; they said of my old district superintendent that he came with ten suits and one sermon.

My district superintendent was known for "radical

preaching." He preached against women wearing makeup, sleeveless blouses, and short hairstyles. I used to admire him a lot; I was indebted to him. But I found out a few years before he died that he was living with another man's wife.

Jesus called this type of legalism "straining out a gnat" while "swallowing a camel" (Matt. 23:24, NIV). Perhaps my old superintendent was not your typical Pharisee because I would like to think that most people who have legalistic tendencies are at least moral men and women. But the funny thing is, this particular man is the very one who told my father that I would "eat dust" because I left my old denomination.

Their Motivations

The Pharisees had a serious problem when it came to money. When Jesus spoke about money (the case can be made that He had more to say about this than anything else), the Pharisees became uncomfortable. When He said, "No one can serve two masters. Either you will hate the one and love the other, or you will be devoted to the one and despise the other. You cannot serve both God and money," the Pharisees "sneered" at Jesus. Luke tells us why: They loved money (Luke 16:13–14, NIV). The King James Version translates *philargyros* as "covetous,"[2] and virtually the same word is used in 1 Timothy 6:10 when Paul said that the "love of money is a root of all kinds of evil." The point is, the Pharisees were motivated by the love of money.

We are talking about the chief enemies of Jesus—who saw right through them. They found their significance in what people said positively about them, by comparing themselves with others, and by their very appearance. I wonder how many preachers today need the good suit or clerical garb just to look successful in order to feel important and significant. If I am not careful, however, I will end up a Pharisee in writing like this, even if unintentionally I suggest that their appearance is an essential ingredient to their sense of significance. But having worn a Geneva gown (a black robe) for the first five years at Westminster Chapel, I know how it feels—a bit more important. Yes, I too just might be a Pharisee.

How do you persuade a Pharisee to give to the poor? The answer is very simple. Hire a couple of trumpeters (a big band would be better) and get everyone's attention with the music. They announced their giving by the sound of trumpets in the synagogues and on the streets for one reason: to be honored by others (Matt. 6:2). And how do you suppose you get a Pharisee to pray? Jesus said, "They love to pray" (v. 5). That is, if it is known to others. If only they loved praying in secret. But no. They wanted it known.

There is nothing wrong with loving to pray. That's good. But the Pharisees loved to pray publicly, standing in synagogues and on street corners where they could be seen by people (v. 5). The way you get them to stop praying is to walk away from them while they are doing it. For their motivation to pray disappears if no one is there to watch and hear them.

And since we know that Pharisees fasted twice a week, what do you suppose lay behind that worthy practice? They made sure you saw them. First, they looked somber, a practice that may not have been too hard for some Pharisees to carry off. Second, they disfigured their faces—they put on a facial expression that told you they were carrying heavy-duty burdens; this was important stuff, mind you. They didn't even comb their hair when they skipped a meal or two because otherwise you might not notice. Read it all in Matthew 6:16–18.

They were starving for attention and recognition. As long as they got credit for giving, praying, or fasting, you could count on them—every time. Take away the credit, the tax exemption, the plaque on the wall, the public knowledge of a generous donation, the thanks before all the doing the flowers in front of the pulpit or for the washing up in the church kitchen and there won't be many lining up wanting to help. Pharisees don't particularly enjoy working behind the scenes, driving someone to church when nobody knows about it, visiting the sick without telling it, or giving until their pockets are empty when only God takes notice.

This reminds me of a time when a lady came up to Louise and me in Fort Lauderdale to say that she had been visiting those who were housebound all week.

"Wonderful," I said. "That's great."

She emphasized she got so much joy in doing this.

"We believe you," we replied.

And then with a straight face she said, "*The greatest joy is in not telling it.*"

The problem with Pharisees is they so often have no objectivity about themselves. This is because their main problem is that they have no sense of sin. None. Sin to them is always in what you do or don't do. Not what you think or feel. It is all outward appearance. They forget that God looks on the heart (1 Sam. 16:7).

Their Priorities

The theological assumptions and priorities of Pharisees can quickly summed up; their theology was more important to them than people. They really didn't care about people. It was all theology. Hold to the truth. Contend for the faith. Keep the party line. Above all, remember the Sabbath. Yes, the Sabbath.

"But my word, dear Pharisee, a blind person was healed."

"Oh yes, but it happened on the Sabbath," comes the terse retort.

"You don't seem to understand. A miracle has taken

place. A person who was born blind and has never seen can now see."

"But you don't understand," says the Pharisee, with as much warmth as you can find in an igloo. "Truth is at stake here. Something has gone terribly wrong if a person is healed on the Sabbath. Therefore, we cannot rejoice when error is clearly being upheld."

Read it for yourself in John 9. Not a single person seemed to be blessed that a blind man could now see. All they could think about was theology. It is almost hilarious that Jesus again and again seemed to wait for the Sabbath before He healed people!

Read Matthew 12:2; Mark 2:24; Luke 6:2, 6; and Luke 14:3 for starters. You get the picture that Jesus sees a needy person but says to Himself, "It's only two more days until the Sabbath is here, and I will wait in order to heal this person then." In other words, Jesus attacked the Pharisees—not for their upholding the Law, but for putting their traditions and party lines alongside Holy Scripture as if they were of the same authority. There isn't a single word in the Law that says a person should not be made well on the Sabbath.

Not only did they not care about people; they "tie up heavy, cumbersome loads and put them on other people's shoulders, but they themselves are not willing to lift a finger to move them" (Matt. 23:4, NIV). They were great at giving orders. They told people what to do. It did not seem to bother them that they could get

people around them to do this. And yet they themselves could not get their hands dirty. This is why
Jesus said, "They do not practice what they preach"
(v. 3, NIV).

How the Pharisees Perpetuated
Their Comfort Zone

You may ask, How could they do this and not feel any
conscience about it? How could they sleep at night?
The answer is what I said above: they had no sense of
sin. To them, sin was not what you think; it was what
you do. This is why Jesus explained the Law in the
Sermon on the Mount as He did: if you hated, you
already committed murder in your heart; if you lusted
after a woman (or caused her to lust), you already
committed adultery in your heart (Matt. 5:21–22, 28).
But they could not see it that way.

This is why they hated all that Jesus preached and
did. He did not hold to the party line. They never
saw their own sin—ever, as far as we can tell. This
is why Jesus said that it was a tax collector, the one
so looked down on by the Pharisee, who was justified before God rather than the Pharisee. "But the tax
collector stood at a distance. He would not even look
up to heaven, but beat his breast and said, 'God, have
mercy on me, a sinner'" (Luke 18:13, NIV).

They further perpetuated their comfort zones by
loopholes they somehow found that set them free from

the kind of obedience they were uncomfortable with. The fences that they erected that supposedly protected the Law actually served in some cases to give a way *not* to obey the Law strictly at all! Jesus nailed them to the wall in this area. The commandment to honor both father and mother was undeniable—this being the fifth of the Ten Commandments. But they had a way of keeping their parents from receiving money that ought to go to them by a rule that enabled them to divert it to the temple or synagogue instead.

> You [Pharisees] say, "If anyone tells his father or his mother, 'What you would have gained from me is given to God,' he need not honor his father." So for the sake of your tradition you have made void the word of God.
> —MATTHEW 15:5–6

When Jesus said that one could not enter the kingdom of heaven unless one's righteousness actually surpassed that of the Pharisee, nobody could believe their ears. The ordinary Jew living at that time thought he or she was so far beneath a Pharisee; the thought of exceeding the righteousness of a Pharisee seemed over the top. But Jesus knew exactly what He was talking about; not only are we justified by faith in Jesus, who perfectly fulfilled the Law on our behalf, but our very righteousness, when we follow Jesus, far outdistances that of the Pharisee. For the Pharisee never felt any conscience about speaking evil of another, hurting the reputation of others, holding a grudge, or not forgiving an enemy.

Jesus knew this. He knew that talk about sin in the heart is what they loathed and despised. (See Matthew 15:10–20.) He taught that it is not what *enters* a person's mouth that makes him unclean; it is what *comes out of it*. It is not what enters the stomach and goes out of the body that defiles the person; it is what comes from the heart that makes them unclean. "For out of the heart come evil thoughts, murder, adultery, sexual immorality, theft, false witness, slander" (v. 19).

Jesus' Doctrine of Sin

What we have here is Jesus' doctrine of sin. You will recall St. Augustine's four stages of humankind; Jesus' doctrine of sin picks up on the second stage: when man after the fall is unable not to sin. Jesus knows that all people are born with original sin; they inherit what Adam became after his fall in the Garden of Eden. We are born with inner depravity. Therefore, it is what is *in the heart of all people* that Jesus is referring to. But sadly the Pharisees did not see this; they emphasized what goes *into* one—food, dieting, keeping certain interpretations of the Law. I think it is safe to say that many Pharisees today emphasize diet and what they eat and forget about what is in the human heart—the things Jesus mentioned, such as murder, adultery, and sexual immorality.

In a word: it is important we see this—Jesus' own doctrine of sin.

When a man or woman has no sense of inward sin, he or she predictably have no objectivity about himself or herself. People like this are utterly blind to their own minds, assumptions, and emotions; they become unteachable. Jesus called them "blind" (Matt. 23:19). A person of mediocre intelligence with a sense of inward sin by the illumination of the Holy Spirit will possess more objectivity about himself or herself and will certainly be easier to live with than a highly educated church member who can only think legalistically and see things as black or white. Blindness to our own sin takes away common sense, basic politeness, and a care for people's feelings. One thing you can surely say about Pharisees—they aren't very nice!

Since Pharisees were vanguards for the Law and were moral and sound on many essential matters, why didn't Jesus congratulate them? Why was He so hard on them? Even if He saw through them, that they were phony in their righteousness, why didn't He leave them alone and attack wicked tax collectors, harlots, and drunkards?

The answer is, Pharisees did so much harm. When they converted a person to their way of thinking, they made that person "twice as much a child of hell" as they were (Matt. 23:15). People like this get more excited over changing a person's theology than they do about leading a person to Christ. They will spend more resources attacking a fellow Christian who threatens them than going into the world to save the lost. It is like King Saul, who was more worried about young David than he was the archenemy of Israel— the Philistines. This is how lopsided people can get and why Jesus knew the Pharisees were dangerous. They did harm to people.

One of the hardest things Jesus said to them was, "You shut the door of the kingdom of heaven in people's faces. You yourselves do not enter, nor will you let those enter who are trying to" (vv. 13–14, NIV). John warned that we must not lose what we have worked for or let someone cause us to lose our reward (2 John 8).

In one of the most heartbreaking moments in my ministry at Westminster Chapel I had to face this kind of issue. There was a man who had been converted through a London mission. He was wonderfully saved and became a part of the family of Westminster Chapel. He had been saved from living in the gutter. It was one of the most wonderful changes of life I have seen.

But parallel with this came difficulties at the Chapel owing to our own evangelism; the influence of Arthur Blessitt led us to singing choruses instead of hymns, reaching the lost by our Pilot Lights program, and my own giving of gentle public invitations on Sunday nights. The result was, sadly, that six of our twelve deacons turned against my ministry. One of the six deacons had befriended this man who had been so gloriously converted through the aforementioned mission. This deacon influenced the new convert. Overnight this new convert turned against the ministry. He began going to another church. The end result was that he did not want to attend church at all and tragically went back to living in the streets.

There is no doubt in my mind that this deacon caused the new convert to lose what he had worked for—as in 2 John 8. He died living in the rough. He will not have lost his salvation (in my opinion) but forfeited a reward at the judgment seat of Christ. And it goes down to the deacon who had influenced this man. Just as Jesus said of the Pharisees: "You shut the kingdom of heaven in people's faces" (Matt. 23:13). They do irreparable damage to innocent people.

This is basically what might have happened to a British couple serving as missionaries in India. They heard that revival had broken out in Wales in 1904. They decided to sail to England in order to go to Wales. After landing in Southampton and arriving in London, they ran into old friends. The latter said to the missionaries, "Whatever are you doing here in London? We thought you were in India."

"We were," the couple from India said, "but we

sailed to England as we want to witness the revival going on in Wales."

The couple said to them, "Don't bother, it is Welsh emotionalism."

"Oh, we didn't realize that." The couple then returned to India without going to Wales, where one of the greatest revivals in the history of Britain took place in 1904–05. I am not saying that the missionaries lost their reward or anything like that, but it shows how people can lose something precious through a Pharisaical type of Christian.

This is why John cautioned: "Watch out that you do not lose what you have worked for, but that you may be rewarded fully" (2 John 8, NIV). This verse is to be applied to one who has made great spiritual progress in their faith—and is well on their way to receiving a reward—but who is still vulnerable to older and "wiser" people who might actually do them harm. Sadly, there are still Pharisees around today who spend more time lecturing zealous new Christians and trying to change their theological views than being concerned about the world going to hell. People like this are usually not soul-winners; they almost always fish in the Christian pond to change one's doctrinal point of view.

Therefore, if you ask, "Why would Jesus not appreciate the Pharisees, but singled them out as enemies when they would seem to be on the right side of the pertinent theological issues?" The answer—again:

they did so much harm. Then and now, Jesus knew they needed to be warned against. On one occasion He compared them with Herod. "Be careful...watch out for the yeast of the Pharisees and that of Herod" (Mark 8:15, NIV). The disciples didn't understand at first, but it eventually sunk in—"he was not telling them to guard against the yeast used in bread, but against the teaching of the Pharisees" (Matt. 16:12, NIV). It, therefore, wasn't personal; they were to guard against the teaching of this people. People are people. But if they imbibe unhealthy teaching, they turn into monsters.

Jesus also knew that the Pharisees would lead the way to His own death. There was never a thought that such a conspiracy would be instigated by the notorious sinners of the day, those who were drunkards, whore-mongers, adulterers, or even murderers. Not that they were incapable of such a crime, but generally speaking, people like that don't tend to send an innocent man to the cross. Religious people do.

Jesus, therefore, had their number and declared war on them from almost the first time He opened His mouth. "Do not think that I have come to abolish the Law," He said early on in the Sermon on the Mount (Matt. 5:17, NIV). Why say that? Why bring the subject up? It was because Jesus wanted to get to the heart of the matter as soon as possible. When He began to attack their interpretations of the Law, He knew He would be in constant battle with them from then on. It worked. They led the way in getting Him crucified. But that is what He came to do! He came to die on the cross for our sins and, in the meantime, establish the kind of people who would be saved. "I have not come to call the righteous [by which He meant those who purport to be righteous], but sinners to repentance" (Luke 5:32, NIV).

What Threatened the Pharisees?

Any success enjoyed by those who did not uphold the Pharisees' party line threatened them. Keep in mind that the Pharisees were a party or sect within Judaism. They wanted prestige and glory for their own party and party line. They feared being outnumbered and were therefore threatened by the common people talking too fondly to Jesus and believing that He was the promised Messiah. This really upset Pharisees. Therefore, when Jesus enjoyed any measure of success (though Jesus was not trying to be "successful" as such)—whether by growing crowds or performing a miracle—the Pharisees were then thrust right out of their comfort zones.

It was basically a matter of jealousy—the sin we never see in ourselves but readily see when others have it. Jealously always intensifies when we are pushed suddenly and without warning outside our comfort zones. When we *choose* to go outside our comfort zones because of obedience to the Lord, it is a different matter; jealousy has greater difficulty growing. But when we are threatened by another's anointing, as Saul was threatened by David (1 Sam. 18:12), our insecurity grows. Fears spreads from the crowns of our heads to the soles of our feet. This is what was happening to Pharisees every time Jesus opened His mouth or performed another miracle.

Even Pontius Pilate knew that "it was out of self-interest that the chief priests had handed Jesus over to him" (Mark 15:10, NIV). They were threatened by the miracles. They were threatened by Jesus' treatment of the Law and His doctrine of sin. And they were, of course, threatened by not achieving "significance" for themselves from the applause of people. What really got their goat was having to watch someone outside their own party winning the hearts of the people.

As I mentioned, "The common people heard him gladly" (Mark 12:37, KJV). On one occasion (see John 7:45–49), they sent temple guards to bring Jesus in so they could arrest Him, but these guards came back without Jesus. Their exchange is recorded in verses 45–47, NIV.

> The Pharisees...asked them, "Why didn't you bring him in?"
>
> "No one ever spoke the way this man does," the guards replied.

"You mean he has deceived you also?" the Pharisees retorted.

This thrust Pharisees right out of their comfort zone. In verse 49, NIV, they resorted to their theology.

"This mob [the people following Jesus]...knows nothing of the law..."

Their ultimate weapon against common Jews was the threat of putting out of the synagogue anyone who confessed faith in Jesus (John 12:42). The typical ploy of a Pharisee is to motivate by fear.

Their attack lay in the idea of guilt by association. This tactic was used by Pharisees then, and it continues to be used today. If people who are attracted to you—or people you spend time with—are unworthy, theologically inarticulate, not of good stock or respectable credentials, all of you are in the same boat together and should be regarded as being cut out of the same cloth. You are all equally guilty to a Pharisee. You prove your guilt by those with whom you are friendly.

The Pharisee trump card, therefore: criticizing the kind of people allowed to be around Jesus, the quality of people affirming Him, and the background of those who were brought closest to Him. "This man welcomes sinners and eats with them" (Luke 15:2, NIV). This, to the Pharisees, should be enough to indict Jesus as one to be shunned; surely this would cause everybody to turn against Jesus. But it didn't work. Jesus even pleaded guilty to the charge and told several more parables (Luke 15 and 16) to show that the Father loves and welcomes sinners into His family.

Pharisees yesterday and today love to repudiate a person by the quality of people they seek to reach or those who admire them. Jesus surprised everybody by choosing a tax collector to be one of the twelve disciples. That was just not right! The Pharisees, on the other hand, quickly wrote of those who mixed with non-adherents to their party line.

I once received a letter from a man who ended it with these words: "May God have mercy on your soul." I doubt the man really wanted this for me, because I spent time with Yasser Arafat and sought to lead him to Christ. I was charged with guilt by association.

Another example was when one of the closest friends I ever had parted ways with me because I accepted a preaching invitation of which he did not approve. His reason was that it did not make him look good since I was known to be close to him. It did not suit him for me to be seen preaching to that particular group of Christians. Again, it was guilt by association.

But on another occasion, I experienced a different outcome. I had a close ministerial friend at the time who refused to go into a bar to witness for Jesus. "Why?" I asked.

"Because someone might see me go in and think I was there to have a drink."

I said to him, "Surely your life is such that people never question why you would be there. Jesus would not care what people thought but would be right in the middle of that bar."

He eventually took my advice and has since thanked me. He began to see God work in his ministry when he did not worry about his reputation.

Reputation means everything to a Pharisee who is looking over his shoulder all the time to see who is watching. The Pharisees wanted to preserve the Law, their fence around the Law, and the reputation of their forefathers who thought they were the last to see God work powerfully in Israel.

The Pharisees were in their comfort zone when praising the great men of God of the past, but they were threatened by the thought that God was doing something new. The notion that He would be at work today put them right outside their comfort zones.

For many, it is great indeed to hear of the wonderful revivals of the past, of men of God who did marvelous and courageous things two hundred years ago, or perhaps only fifty years ago. But not today. We are in our comfort zones talking about what God did yesterday. But talk of God doing something today, unless it is on some remote island in the Third World, is too threatening a topic. Anyone who says that what is happening now is of God will be treated with disbelief.

This was part of the offense when Jesus stood and read from Isaiah 61:1–2, then sat down and declared, "*Today* this scripture is fulfilled in your hearing" (Luke 4:18–21, NIV, emphasis added). It was of great offense when Peter, speaking on the day of Pentecost, said that what was going on before their very eyes was the fulfillment of the prophet Joel's words (Acts 2:16–21). Any reckoning that God is at work *now* makes us all uneasy; but Pharisaism behind the surface breaks out in fear and suspicion.

Pharisees are even threatened by those who actually do not pose a threat to them at all—for example, children. The ire of self-righteousness will rise in the Pharisee when children lose their heads and get involved in worshipping Jesus. This happened on Palm Sunday. "But when the chief priests and the teachers of the law saw the wonderful things he did and the children shouting in the temple courts, 'Hosanna to the Son of David,' they were indignant" (Matt. 21:15, NIV).

What do children know? How much theological training could they have received? What's more, these children were shouting! That sort of thing always makes religious people uneasy. When we see kids—or any young person—getting carried away under the inspiration of worship and praise, we get very uncomfortable. We are afraid things will get out of hand.

I have watched God move powerfully over the years when children get involved. I have often thought that the next move of God on earth will witness children and young people doing mighty things for the Lord—possibly even leading the way.

How They Reacted

When a Pharisee is outside his comfort zone, he has to do something. One of the main things he does is accuse and say, "This is not of God." Sometimes he crosses over a line and says, "This is of the devil." This is a dangerous thing to do. When this was done in the presence of Jesus and the miraculous, He introduced a very scary teaching—the sin for which there is no forgiveness. He called it blasphemy against the Holy Spirit, which makes a person guilty of an "eternal sin"—all because they were saying of Jesus, "He has an impure spirit" (Mark 3:28–30, NIV).

Why is it that some of us are more willing to believe the devil is at work than that something or someone is actually of God? If we have a party line that says, "God does not do the miraculous nowadays—that ended after the closing of the canon of Scripture," we are forced to explain what is happening. To be on the safe side we might say a miracle takes place by psychological reaction.

This was said when my wife, Louise, in her weakest and darkest hour, was prayed for by Rodney

Howard-Browne and was instantaneously healed. I know of some who accused Rodney of preaching in a tongue that was demonic and out of the dark regions of Africa. Whoever said it first, I don't know; I only know I would not want to be in their shoes.

It is one thing to be outside your comfort zone because of reports of the miraculous that you don't understand; it is crossing well over the line to say it is of Satan. Whatever you say, don't say that.

It is sad but sobering to realize how far we will go to defend our party line. We get defensive. Say crazy things. Get very suspicious. Send out spies. Like those Jews who were sent from Jerusalem to investigate John the Baptist (John 1:19). Anyone who puts us outside our comfort zone—such as a man wearing clothes made of camel's hair and calling for repentance—becomes our next target.

Before it is all over we even turn on the man who was actually healed. That's what happened to the lad who was healed of blindness. Though he ought to have had a chance to enjoy his sight for a little while, he was instead having to explain himself and was eventually persecuted—just because he was the one healed (John 9:26–34).

Pharisees who are thrust outside their comfort zones seem to live for the moment when they can trap the one who threatens them, touch them in an unguarded moment, or find something that enables them to say "Gotcha!" What a way to live: using your time and energy to hope someone will make a comment by which they can be labeled heretic or, at least, be embarrassed.

Pharisees yesterday and today live for this. "Then the Pharisees went out and laid plans to trap him in his words" (Matt. 22:15, NIV). When they found the woman in the act of adultery, they used their questions about her "as a trap, in order to have basis for accusing him" (John 8:3–6, NIV). They hope for the moment they can catch someone and make him or her lose face. People like this are not happy with themselves and will continue on unless God mercifully reaches down and touches their hearts—as in the case of Nicodemus or Saul of Tarsus. That means there is hope for all of us who are plagued by Pharisaical weakness.

The worst thing of all, however, was this. The Pharisees' search for significance outside God and from the praise of people lay at the bottom of their inability to recognize God's Messiah when He stood before their very eyes. Have you wondered why ancient Israel missed out when the Messiah came? Have you wondered why they still reject Him? I can tell you. It is because they chose the immediate gratification of receiving praise from people rather than to seek honor that comes only from God.

Seeking the honor, praise, and glory that comes from God alone means letting go of the applause of men and women. It also means having a lot of patience, because you don't feel anything the first day when you make this a lifelong pursuit. So it isn't easy.

The Pharisees simply weren't going to go that route; it was too hard. Surely their reverence for the Law was good enough. The Law is God's product; the Law isn't God Himself. And those who give priority to the Law inevitably end up as Pharisees and miss out on God's next move, just as the Jews missed out on their own Messiah.

Therefore, Jesus was not surprised at their refusal to believe in Him. He gave the explanation Himself and summed up their unbelief in a simple question: "How can you believe since you accept glory from one another but do not seek the glory that comes from the only God?" (John 5:44, NIV). They made a choice: they preferred compliments, adoration, admiration, and glory from people.

Jesus said they made no effort to see what it would have been like had they sought their significance in the sheer glory of God. Instead, they opted for the glory of man. This felt better, possibly, for a while. But at the end of the day one who makes this choice will pay for it dearly and suffer for it bitterly—forever—unless God mercifully steps in, as He did in the case of Nicodemus and Saul of Tarsus. And me. And I hope you.

It breaks my heart that the Pharisees were the ones

who led to Jesus weeping over the city of Jerusalem in a lengthy denunciation of the Pharisees in Matthew 23. It culminates in Jesus crying out,

> Jerusalem, Jerusalem, you who kill the prophets and stone those sent to you, how often I have longed to gather your children together, as a hen gathers her chicks under her wings, but you were not willing. Look, your house is left to you desolate.
>
> —MATTHEW 23:37–38, NIV

CHAPTER 4

The Sense of Sin

*If we say we have no sin, we deceive ourselves,
and the truth is not in us.*

—1 JOHN 1:8

THE PHARISEES HAD no sense of sin. Do you have a sense of sin? If not, it is not a good sign. Caution: you just might be a Pharisee!

There was a time when I sincerely believed I lived above sin. This was before my baptism of the Holy Spirit that took place on October 31, 1955, while driving in my car one Monday morning in Tennessee. The person of Jesus was more real to me than anyone or anything around me. I was utterly changed that day. However, this teaching of living without sinning had been drummed in me from my mother's knee, and since I had not killed anybody, stolen, lied, or committed fornication, I assumed I was without sin.

Sometime after this experience of the Holy Spirit, I read 1 John 1:8 as though for the first time. I was immediately convicted. A sense of sinfulness emerged in me. Had I been guilty of any particular sin, such as murder or adultery? No. Lying? No. Stealing? No. But the words of John gripped me, and a sense of sinfulness set in my heart. That is what 1 John 1:8 did for me.

Understanding the tenth commandment, "You shall not covet" (Exod. 20:17; Rom. 7:7), is what did it for Paul. He had previously felt that he was without sin. But when he saw the depth of the meaning of coveting, he said that "sin came alive and I died" (Rom. 7:9). He realized he had indeed coveted things! What made him covet? Sin in him.

First John 1:8 does not say we have no sin; it says, "If we *say* we have no sin, we deceive ourselves and the truth is not in us." And I had been making that very claim, namely, *saying* that I had no sin. I now had to make a choice: agree that 1 John 1:8 was the infallible Word of God and admit that I had sin or set myself above Holy Scripture.

I realized I had been sinning by *saying or claiming* or *believing* I had no sin. The sense of sin at last set in, and I was never the same again.

To be fair to myself, I had been hung up on the meaning of the word *cleanse* in 1 John 1:7. It says that "the blood of Jesus...cleanses us from all sin." And certain teachers in my background made the claim that *cleanse* means to eradicate sin as if sin is a tangible substance that has been pulled up by the roots and no longer exists. They said that makes us without sin.

That is *not* what John is saying, and it is the very reason he follows 1 John 1:7 with verse 8, which warns us from saying we have no sin. Then what does *cleanse* mean? Answer: that we who have been cleansed can feel pure and enjoy fellowship with the Father as if there were no sin at all; that we who have been purified can truly feel—experience—His immediate and direct presence. These verses in 1 John do not refer to "head knowledge" or theory; he is talking about experiencing the Holy Spirit. God *sees* us as clean, and we can *feel* clean, yet we are conscious that sin is there.

To demonstrate how my background had a hold on me by making me think I was above sin, consider the beloved hymn, "Come Thou Fount of Every Blessing." The last part of the third verse of this great hymn says,

> Prone to wander, Lord I feel it,
>
> prone to leave the God I love;
>
> here's my heart, O take and seal it,
>
> seal it for thy courts above.[1]
>
> —ROBERT ROBINSON (1735–1790)

My old denomination might have omitted the hymn from their official hymnal. Instead, they wanted to keep it but change what they didn't like. Whereas their hymnal quotes the author's lyrics verbatim throughout the hymn, the church leaders felt they had to change that last part of verse three. Instead of singing, "Prone to wander, Lord I feel it, prone to leave the God I love," here is what they inserted that I had been singing all my life:

> Let me know Thee in Thy fullness;
>
> Guide me by Thy mighty hand
>
> Till, transformed, in Thine own image
>
> In Thy presence I shall stand.[2]
>
> —Praise and Worship: The Nazarene
> Hymnal, 1951

The irony here is that those who changed the words probably felt they did not sin by doing so! They did it so they could keep this immortal hymn in their hymnals but still protect their doctrine! As I said, they could have omitted the hymn from their hymnal altogether. But no. They changed the author's words and, by doing so, fostered their theological belief that we may live above sin.

After coming to a sense of sin, I never lost my desire

to live a holy life. A life of holiness—and doing my best to live without sinning—continued to be paramount to me. Let no one think that this sense of sin means we are now free to sin and that we now live sinful lives. The result is the opposite of that.

I used to wonder why it was that the greatest saints in church history always saw themselves as the greatest sinners. Now I began to understand that.

What changed my own understanding of sin was two things: (1) my baptism of the Spirit and (2) being convicted by 1 John 1:8. That I could see my sin showed that the truth was in me! I had missed the most salient point of all that John makes in 1 John 1:7: sin in us remains, but we are purified by walking in the light of God. The sin is *there,* but it is *forgiven* and does not haunt us or make us feel guilty. We feel free because we are free. The cleansing blood enables us to feel pure while we know at the same time there is a propensity in us to wander from God.

Strange as this may seem, it is exactly what is true: we feel clean yet conscious of a weakness. This is why Paul could say, "Let anyone who thinks that he stands take heed lest he fall" (1 Cor. 10:12). This is also why John warned against claiming we have no sin. If you say you have no sin, you are close to saying you are glorified—which is what will happen in heaven. When we are glorified it will not be possible to sin because there will be no sin in us! But because there is sin in us now, we are continually conscious we could displease the Lord.

This is what Nicolas Herman (1614–1691), known as Brother Lawrence, felt all the time. He enjoyed the direct presence of God but was perpetually conscious of his weakness and proneness to sin.

By contrast, the Pharisees had no sense of their own sin at all. It did not enter into their thinking. Such a concept and such a feeling was remote to them. This then is the way Paul, brought up as a Pharisee, felt until he realized what the tenth commandment—you shall not covet—meant.

Six Things About Sin

There are six things we need to see about the knowledge of sin.

1. The purpose of the Law

The purpose of the Law was twofold. First, through fear of punishment it restrained sin. It was brought in because of the transgressions of Israel (Gal. 3:19). The sinning of ancient Israel got out of hand. The Mosaic Law was brought in. It did not completely stop people from sinning, but it nonetheless had the effect of slowing it down. How? Through fear of punishment. The fear of punishment works.

Years ago in London, I parked my car in a spot reserved for ambassadors. As it was a Saturday afternoon, I then spent a couple of hours working on a sermon in my old *bolt-hole* (quiet place). When I came out, the car was gone! It had been towed away. The cost to get the car—plus the fine—was horrendous. But I never parked my car there again! Fear of punishment works!

Second, the Law names what sin is. That is why we have the Ten Commandments; it spells out what sin is, e.g., idolatry, murder, adultery, stealing. Through the Law we have the knowledge of sin (Rom. 3:20; 7:7). Sin existed from the day Adam fell. Adultery was a sin before the Law came in (Rom. 5:13) and was regarded as sin before the Law came in (Gen. 39:9). What the Law did, then, was to identify wrongdoing so that one was told specifically what sin was.

The Mosaic Law may be understood as (1) Moral Law (the Ten Commandments), (2) Civil Law (the way the people of Israel should be governed), and (3) Ceremonial Law (the way God wants to be worshipped). The Ceremonial Law includes the sacrificial system—the shedding of blood of animals, particularly lambs or bulls—which I will discuss next.

2. The purpose of the sacrificial system

This system is part of the Ceremonial Law and shows how God wants to be worshipped. Because we are sinners, we need a sacrifice. Christ's death on the cross was the ultimate fulfillment of the sacrificial system. The shedding of blood reveals the justice of

God and the seriousness of sin. Dr. D. James Kennedy (1930–2007) in his "Evangelism Explosion" program used to say that the Bible basically says two things about God: (1) that He is a God of justice (that sin must be punished) and (2) that He is a God of mercy, which means He does not want to punish us. But before He can show mercy, His justice must be satisfied. God's justice means that He must punish sin. The way sin is punished is by the slaughtering of a lamb or a bull. Sin had to be punished. It required the shedding of blood.

But why the shedding of blood? It is because God is angry with sin. God brought in the sacrificial system to teach Israel that sin infinitely offends the Most Holy God. The only way God begins to be pacified is by the substitutionary death of an innocent animal. If sin were not serious and infinitely offensive, then trying to keep the Moral Law by good works would be sufficient. One would satisfy God by keeping the works of the Law. This is exactly what the Pharisees believed: they atoned by good works. This is what Rabbi David Rosen believes will save him, as seen in our book *The Christian and the Pharisee.*

The problem was that no one kept the Law. Furthermore, the shedding of the blood of an animal did not fully satisfy God's justice. The proof of this is that the offerings had to be repeated—again and again and again. Hebrews chapter ten pointed to the need of an ultimate sacrifice.

Therefore, the sacrificial system was but a shadow of things to come. This is the essential point that the writer of Hebrews makes.

> For since the law has but a shadow of the good things to come instead of the true form of these realities, it can never, by the same sacrifices that are continually offered year after year, make perfect those who draw near. Otherwise, would they not have ceased to be offered, since the worshippers, having once been cleansed, would no longer have any consciousness of sins? But in these sacrifices there is a reminder of sins every year. For it is impossible for the blood of bulls and goats to take away sins.
> —HEBREWS 10:1–4

The bottom line: the sacrificial system shows the seriousness of sin—how God hates it—and how God's wrath is not appeased by the shedding of the blood of animals. This is why God sent His Son—a human being—into the world. "For God so loved the world, that he gave his only Son, that whoever believes in him should not perish but have eternal life" (John 3:16). In giving His Son, God the Father punished Jesus for what we did. On Good Friday, sometime between noon and three o'clock, God poured out His wrath on Jesus. This was why Jesus cried out "My God, my God, why have you forsaken me?" (Matt. 27:46). Paul summed it up: "For our sake he made him to be sin who knew no sin, so that in him we might become the righteousness of God" (2 Cor. 5:21).

But the Jews generally, particularly the Pharisees, missed this entirely. They did not see sin as a problem. They focused on their good works and impressing the people around them. As I've mentioned, they lived for praise—not for the praise of God but the praise of men. Jesus, therefore, gave the reason that they did not believe in Him: "How can you believe, when you receive glory from one another and do not seek the glory that comes from the only God?" (John 5:44).

Because they were blind to their own sin, the Pharisees did not think it was a failure that they desired the praise of each other rather than God's honor. They should have been the first to see the utter importance of the honor of God. But their love for the praise of people was their downfall. Consequently, the Pharisees did not see that it was the seriousness of sin that required the sacrificial system. In any case, that they kept up with the sacrifices made them feel satisfied. The liturgy blinded them. Parallel with this was their own blindness to sin generally and to their personal failings.

3. The purpose of the Sermon on the Mount

The Sermon on the Mount had more than one purpose—not necessarily in this order. First, to show that the kingdom of heaven is not something visible but instead exists in the hearts of people. This was one of the more difficult concepts for the disciples to grasp. In fact, they never twigged to the meaning until the Holy Spirit fell on the day of Pentecost. That said, Jesus said all that could be said at the time. He told them that the kingdom of God (the same, by the way, as the kingdom of heaven) was not visible—like you expect of an earthly kingdom.

> The kingdom of God is not coming in ways that can be observed, nor will they say, "Look, here it is!" or "There!" for behold, the kingdom of God is in the midst of you [or within you].
> —Luke 17:20–21

Despite these words the notion of a visible, physical kingdom was the way the disciples continued to envisage the kingdom. Even after Jesus was raised from the dead, they asked, "Lord, will you at this time restore the kingdom to Israel?" (Acts 1:6). They could not conceive of a kingdom in any other way. They got it when the Spirit came down on the day of Pentecost.

And yet all that Jesus said about the kingdom showed that it was something that is in people's *hearts*. That is what the entire Sermon on the Mount is about.

Second, the Sermon on the Mount was preached to show the kind of righteousness the kingdom of heaven requires, namely, righteousness that exceeds—or surpasses—the righteousness of the Pharisees. This topic is so important that I am devoting an entire chapter—Chapter 5—to the kind of righteousness that surpasses that of the Pharisees.

Its third purpose was to unveil Jesus' doctrine of the Holy Spirit. In fact, the Sermon on the Mount will never be truly understood until we see it as an unveiling of the Holy Spirit. True, the Holy Spirit is not explicitly mentioned in the Sermon on the Mount. But neither is God or the Lord mentioned in the Book of Esther—one of the most God-centered books in Scripture.

Fourth, the Sermon on the Mount demonstrates the true nature of sin. This comes parallel with Jesus' teaching of the righteousness that surpasses—or outclasses—that of the Pharisees.

Fifth, the Sermon on the Mount shows why Jesus came to the world, namely, to die on a cross for our sins. In a word, it points to the cross of Jesus. When Jesus said He had come to fulfill the Law (Matt. 5:17), it pointed to His sinless life and sacrificial death on the cross. I will cover more about this later in this book.

If you would like to understand more about the Beatitudes, kingdom righteousness, or the whole of this amazing Sermon, I have written an entire exposition titled *The Sermon on the Mount.*[3]

4. The work of the Holy Spirit

After Jesus introduced the Holy Spirit to the disciples, He said,

> And when he comes, he will convict the world concerning sin and righteousness and judgment: concerning sin because they do not believe in me; concerning righteousness, because I go to the Father, and you will see me no longer; concerning judgment, because the ruler of this world is judged.
>
> —JOHN 16:8–11

The first thing the Holy Spirit would do, then, is to convict the world of sin. The world refers to those not saved; the Holy Spirit paves the way for people being saved by making them see they have sinned. They need to see that they need to be saved. People don't know they have a need until they are awakened by the Spirit. They feel perfectly fine in themselves until God wakes them up. They are given the gospel message that God sent His Son into the world to die for our sins. That is why He came. But to appreciate this requires people seeing themselves as lost; otherwise, they would not see the need of a Savior.

Jesus also said that no one can come to Him unless drawn by the Father (John 6:44). The Father drawing one refers to the work of the Holy Spirit. We are born "dead in the trespasses and sins" (Eph. 2:1). We are born dead! This means that, spiritually speaking, we are born dead. A dead person cannot move; he or she cannot see or hear.

Paul reminded the Ephesians that they were born this way. What changed them? "But God, being rich in mercy, because of the great love in which he loved us, even when we were dead in our trespasses, made us alive together with Christ—by grace you have been saved" (Eph. 2:4–5).

What happens is this. The Holy Spirit applies the truth as one hears the gospel. Had not the Holy Spirit intervened when the gospel was being preached, no one would be saved.

Consider Saul of Tarsus. On the day of his conversion he was not on his way to a Billy Graham meeting to hear preaching. He was determined to kill Christians. But he had heard the gospel. He heard what Stephen preached in Acts chapter 7. The Spirit began to speak then, although no one would have thought it. He headed on his journey to arrest Christians. But something was going on inside of him. Jesus said to him, "It is hard for you to kick against the goads" (Acts 26:14). This means that Saul was trying to resist the wooing of the Spirit and kept on trying to carry out his mission to arrest Christians. But God was at work in him; Saul finally caved in and said, "What shall I do, Lord?" (Acts 22:10).

This was truly an extraordinary, dramatic conversion. And yet my old mentor Rolfe Barnard preached an unforgettable sermon called, "Paul's Conversion: A Normal Conversion." In this sermon Rolfe showed how no one would be saved apart from the sovereign work of the Holy Spirit. This is absolutely true. One may not see this at first. But in time, if he or she reflects on his or her conversion very deeply, he or she will see it is what God did.

Indeed, the preacher Charles Spurgeon tells how he was sitting in a Methodist church, pondering his own conversion. "Why did I believe?" he asked himself. "I believed because I heard the word—when suddenly I saw that God was at the bottom of it all, that it was all of grace."

Heaven will be filled with people who realize throughout eternity they have no right to be there. We will be aware that we are in heaven by the sheer grace of God. "For by grace you have been saved through faith. And this is not your doing; it is the gift of God, not a result of works, so that no one may boast" (Eph. 2:8–9). Dr. Martyn Lloyd-Jones always said that a Christian is a person who is "surprised" that he is a Christian; one is conscious that he or she is a work of sovereign grace.

5. The sensitivity of the Holy Spirit

I wrote a book entitled *The Sensitivity of the Holy Spirit.* I regard my insight into this truth as perhaps the most important and deepest of my entire ministry. The purpose of that book is to show that the Holy Spirit—the third Person of the Trinity—is a very, very sensitive person. This means He is easily grieved (Eph. 4:30). But that is not all; if we become knowledgeable of His ways, we will become sensitive to what grieves Him, namely, sin. Sin we had not seen in ourselves. The work of the Holy Spirit is to reveal sin; yes, to the world first. But He continues to do this in the heart and life of the believer, that is, one who listens to the Spirit's voice.

> As the Holy Spirit says, "Today, if you hear his voice, do not harden your hearts as in the rebellion, on the day of testing in the wilderness, where your fathers put me to the test and saw my works for forty years. Therefore I was provoked with that generation, and said, 'They always go astray in their heart; they have not known my ways.'"
>
> —Hebrews 3:7–10

As a consequence of this, God swore in His wrath, "They shall not enter my rest" (v. 11).

What we learn from this account of ancient Israel, as told in the Epistle to the Hebrews, is that true believers can be guilty of not listening to the Spirit's voice. Yes, those Israelites were true believers. Never doubt this. They were the ones who kept the Passover in Egypt, obeying Moses (Exod. 12:28). They were the ones who crossed the Red Sea on dry land (Exod. 14:29). Indeed, they "feared the LORD, and they believed in the LORD and in his servant Moses" (Exod. 14:31). Paul drives home the fact that they *all* were believers: "our fathers were *all* under the cloud, and *all* passed through the sea, and *all* were baptized into Moses in the cloud and in the sea, and *all* ate the same spiritual food, and *all* drank from the spiritual Rock that followed them, and the Rock was Christ" (1 Cor. 10:1–4, emphasis added).

Christians who do not become sensitive to the Holy Spirit's ways—and do not repent when their sin is shown to them—*repeat what happened to ancient Israel.* In a word: they blow away their inheritance. Israel should have inherited the Promised Land— Canaan. But God was not pleased "with most of them" (1 Cor. 10:5). God swore in His wrath that they would *not* enter into His rest.

They were saved, yes. They will be in heaven, yes. But, because they grieved the Holy Spirit by their sin and unbelief in the desert, they forfeited their inheritance.

Every Christian is called to come into his or her inheritance. Some do, some don't. As the late Michael

Eaton would say, "Inheritance is what you get by persistent faith." Those who do come into their inheritance will receive a reward at the judgment seat of Christ (1 Cor. 3:14). Anyone who doesn't will "suffer loss" of reward, but will "be saved, but only as through fire" (v. 15).

It comes down to whether we will develop a consciousness of sin, of what grieves the Holy Spirit. The chief way we grieve the Spirit is by bitterness and unforgiveness. This is why Paul follows this warning about grieving the Spirit of God with these words.

> Let all bitterness and wrath and anger and clamor and slander be put away from you, along with all malice. Be kind to one another, tenderhearted, forgiving one another, as God in Christ forgave you.
>
> —Ephesians 4:31–32

I'm sorry, but there are many Christians—yes, true Christians—who do not take these words seriously when it comes to forgiveness. I wrote the book *Total Forgiveness,* which speaks to the greatest problem in the church today. How is it that we can hold a grudge, excuse our unforgiveness, and carry on without the slightest feeling of guilt or shame?

I will answer that. I'm sorry and very ashamed to admit it, but that was the way I lived for years. Holding a grudge did not bother me. I dismissed Jesus' words about loving your enemy and forgiving people by assuming "none of us is perfect" and "we all sin." But thankfully God in mercy—I am tempted to say extreme mercy—sent Josif Tson into my life. It was a wake-up call: "R. T., you must totally forgive them. Until you totally forgive them, you will be in chains. Forgive them, and you will be released." I die a thousand deaths when I think of how the rest of my life might have turned out had not God sent Josif Tson to me.

I have preached my sermon "Total Forgiveness" all over the world—almost entirely to Christians. When I give the invitation for people to stand because they need to forgive—and thus promise that they will forgive—often at least *90 percent* of the congregation will stand. Why? Because they needed to be converted? Possibly some of them. But I would say that most of them are truly saved people. In fact it has been my observation that the most spiritual are the quickest to stand up and forgive!

My point is this. Many people who are truly saved—born again—need to hear the voice of the Holy Spirit like the ancient Israelites. If they persist in unforgiveness, they will blow away their inheritance—as I most certainly was in danger of doing.

In a word: the conscientious Christian will earnestly take care not to grieve the Holy Spirit. The result of the Spirit's work in us will be to sense sin—which needs to be confessed (1 John 1:9). First John 1:7 says that the blood of Christ cleanses us when we walk in the light; 1 John 1:8 cautions us not to say we have no sin; 1 John 1:9 is the sweet invitation to be forgiven by confessing our sins. Note: 1 John 1:9 was not written to lost people; it was written to Christians: "If we confess our sins, he is faithful and just to forgive us our sins and to cleanse us from all unrighteousness."

6. Seeing the glory of God

Isaiah had been serving the Lord and prophesying for a good while before he said one day: "Woe is me! For I am lost; for I am a man of unclean lips" (Isa. 6:5). Whatever does this mean? By *lost* does he mean he was not saved? That he did not even know the Lord? I don't think that is what he meant. I believe it is the way he honestly *felt*. What caused this? Answer: one day he saw the glory of the Lord like he had never experienced it before.

> In the year that king Uzziah died, I saw the LORD sitting upon a throne, high and lifted up; and the train of his robe filled the temple. Above him stood the seraphim. Each had six wings: with two he covered his face, and with two he covered his feet, and with two he flew. And one called to another and said:
>
>> "Holy, holy, holy is the LORD of hosts;

the whole earth is full of
his glory!"

And the foundations of the thresholds shook at
the voice of him who called, and the house was
filled with smoke. And I said: "Woe is me! For
I am lost; for I am a man of unclean lips, and
I dwell in the midst of a people of unclean lips;
for my eyes have seen the King, the LORD of
hosts!"

—ISAIAH 6:1–5

Isaiah had what one might reasonably call a post-conversion experience. It was truly an experience of the Holy Spirit. It changed his life; he was never to be the same again. The immediate result of this experience was that he felt sinful. Dirty. Unclean.

My friend Arthur Blessitt told me of a time he was in Lake Tahoe, Nevada. This was long before he began his ministry in Hollywood, long before he became a well-known preacher. At age twenty-three, he and a friend named Ron felt led to go to the lake and pray. Arthur said there was snow on the ground, and it was cold. Arthur related to me that, as they were praying, "I saw Him. It was Jesus walking on the lake." He then said to Ron, who was praying with him, "Do you see what I see?" His friend replied, "Yes." Arthur said to him, "Let's make sure we are truly seeing what we think we are. That we haven't lost our minds. We see this tree. We see the casinos in a distance. We know we are here by this lake. Now let us turn together and look and see if He is still there."

They turned and looked. There Jesus was, walking on the lake. "He started to walk toward us," Arthur said to me. "The closer He got, the worse I felt. I felt so dirty. If you had wiped human dung on my face, I would not have felt worse. I felt so awful. And then I began to cry out, 'Bless me, Jesus, bless me, Jesus, bless me, Jesus.' He was about fifteen feet away. He looked at me and smiled. And suddenly I felt a peace like I had never felt; I then felt clean and pure. He looked at me and smiled. I felt waves of glory coming over me. And He was gone."

I believe Arthur's story. Arthur is now seventy-nine. I don't think he is well physically. Why would he have felt so dirty, so unclean? This to me confirmed the authenticity of this story. For what it's worth, my having Arthur Blessitt at Westminster Chapel was the best decision I made in my twenty-five years there. His impact on me cannot be fully described.

Arthur's experience is similar to that of a man I once talked with who had seen true revival in Uganda, Africa. He said that there was a time when "we lost all consciousness of people around us. The presence of God was so real that we did not think about others' thoughts. We felt so sinful that we literally beat our chests with a feeling of conviction of sin."

In the Old Testament, the prophet Malachi said, "the Lord whom you seek will suddenly come to his temple." But he then added, "who can endure the day of his coming, and who can stand when he appears? For he is like a refiner's fire and like fullers' soap. He will sit as a refiner and a purifier of silver" (Mal. 3:1–3).

There was more to Isaiah's vision of the glory of the Lord: "Then one of the seraphim flew to me, having in his hand a burning coal that he had taken with tongs from the altar. And he touched my mouth and said: 'Behold, this has touched your lips; your guilt is taken away, and your sin atoned for'" (Isa. 6:6–7).

God does not show us our sin merely to make us feel guilty and shameful; He does it to show us how terrible sin is but that it can be forgiven.

The worst possible state to be in is to say, "We have no sin." Do you feel like that? Caution: you just may be a Pharisee.

CHAPTER 5

The Righteousness That Exceeds That of the Pharisees

For I tell you, unless your righteousness exceeds
that of the scribes and Pharisees, you will never
enter the kingdom of heaven.

—MATTHEW 5:20

Y OU MAY RECALL that one of the purposes of the Sermon on the Mount was to show what is meant by righteousness that exceeds the righteousness of the Pharisees. Incredible as this may seem at first, it becomes quickly clear once we grasp what Jesus meant.

One of the main things for us to see in this book and in this chapter is how true righteousness *really* exceeds—or surpasses—that of the Pharisees. One's first question is likely to be, How can this be? Surely the Pharisees were seen as the ultimate holy, pious, and lawful people who were careful not to break the Law and who also came up with rules that went beyond the Law so that they would be less likely to break the Law itself! How could one's righteousness go beyond that?

The answer is: we are talking about an inward righteousness, not external.

There are actually two ways our righteousness exceeds that of the Pharisees: (1) imputed righteousness—by faith in Christ's blood—and (2) imparted righteousness—that comes by persistent faith. Imputed righteousness is what gets us to heaven; imparted righteousness is what gets us our inheritance. One act of faith in the blood of Christ rather than our works is what saves us. When we transfer the trust we had in our good works to what Jesus did for us on the cross, the righteousness of Jesus—His life and death—is put to our credit. This is imputed righteousness. It is what saves us. But although once saved, always saved, we must nonetheless continue in the faith that secures our inheritance—as Colossians 2:6–7 puts it: "As you received Christ Jesus the Lord, so walk in him, rooted and built up in him and established in the faith." Persistent faith is what gets us our inheritance. Persistent faith is what enables us to demonstrate the righteousness that exceeds—surpasses or outclasses—the righteousness of the Pharisees.

It Begins With the Beatitudes

Jesus laid the groundwork for His teaching on exceeding the righteousness of the Pharisees in the Beatitudes. From the opening comment, "Blessed are the poor in spirit, for theirs is the kingdom of heaven" (Matt. 5:3), a righteousness that was alien to the Pharisees had begun to be described.

The language in the Beatitudes—Matthew 5:3–12—was very likely Jesus' "text" for all He said in the Sermon on the Mount. All that followed the Beatitudes—Matthew 5:13–7:27—was an exposition of Matthew 5:3–12.

I have been to the very spot—or within a few feet—where Jesus preached the Sermon on the Mount. It is very interesting. There is a flat area immediately north of the Sea of Galilee not far from Capernaum—a level space of several yards—where Jesus initially stood (Luke 6:17), then sat (Matt. 5:1). I have stood there and read from Matthew 5 while my friend Lyndon Bowring sat on the rising hill that provided a convenient place for people to sit as if it were a stadium—for hundreds and hundreds of hearers. Lyndon could hear every word I read. The acoustics were perfect for such an event.

The hill explains how Jesus "came down with them

and stood on a level place" (Luke 6:17). In other words, there was a level place where Jesus spoke; before Him was a rising hill, or mountain; behind Him one went down a hill toward the Sea of Galilee. If one is near the Sea of Galilee and looks at the spot where Jesus taught, it is a mountain, just as the Bible says. The Bible does not contradict itself. Yes, Jesus came down from a mountain and stood; and yet the Sermon on the Mountain is up on a large hill rising from the Sea of Galilee. Archaeologists—even recognized by the modern state of Israel—have established this as a fact.

Some think Matthew's account and Luke's account show that Jesus preached this sermon twice. While that is possible, it is more likely that it is one event. That said, Dr. Michael Eaton thinks Jesus probably taught this over a period of three or four days, that what we have in Matthew and Luke provide a summary of Jesus' sermon. It is probably also true that Peter's sermon on the day of Pentecost (Acts 2:14–36) lasted an hour or more, that Luke gives us a summary of it.

Here is my summary of the Beatitudes: The word *blessed* comes from *makarios,* which means happy. Some say it should be translated "congratulations," and I agree. These Beatitudes immediately point to a righteousness that exceeds that of the Pharisees. These Beatitudes also point to a rising scale of holiness and discipline; each level shows more godly progress in the kingdom of heaven.

Congratulations to:

- "The poor in spirit," namely, those who know they are spiritually bankrupt; they realize they have no bargaining power with God; they can only plead for His mercy. The kingdom of heaven belongs to people like this and not those who have a feeling of entitlement.

- "Those who mourn"; those conscious of their sinfulness, but also those who mourn for any reason—Jesus is there to be with them in grief. Such people will know His comfort.

- "The meek," those who turn the cheek instead of defending themselves when insulted; they shall inherit the earth— to be the head not the tail in God's kingdom.

- "Those who hunger and thirst for righteousness"—a desire that has no natural explanation; they want all that God has in mind for them and will not be disappointed.

- "The merciful," those who are like their heavenly Father who has mercy for all; instead of getting even with those who mistreat them, they totally forgive their enemies.

- "The pure in heart," those who are single-minded in wanting God's will, including sexual purity; they are the ones who will see God's glory in the here and now.

- "The peacemakers," those who not only succeed in getting enemies to start speaking to each other; they risk losing friends because they know they can lose them by lovingly asking them to forgive. Such people are God's children.

- "Those persecuted for righteousness' sake," not those who suffer owing to their selfish and strange ways but who have stood for the principles of the glory of God. Congratulations: you belong to the kingdom of heaven.

- "Those who are persecuted for righteousness' sake" are not only happy but to be congratulated; you belong to a great company—those Old Testament prophets of long ago.

Therefore when Jesus said, "For I tell you, unless your righteousness exceeds that of the scribes and Pharisees, you will never enter the kingdom of heaven" (Matt. 5:20), it becomes apparent what He means by that. At first glance of the notion of exceeding the righteousness of Pharisees, people could not imagine how *anyone* could enter the kingdom! And surely nobody surpasses the righteousness of the holy Pharisees! But Jesus' explanation makes this clear. What He says next in the Sermon on the Mount explains why He started with the Beatitudes.

Jesus chose to focus on three of the Ten Commandments: (1) the sixth—"You shall not murder" (Matt. 5:21–26, 43–48); (2) the seventh—"You shall not commit adultery" (Matt. 5:27–30); and (3) the third commandment, which pertains to the misuse of God's name (Matt. 5:33–37).

The sixth command, "You shall not murder" (Exod. 20:13), as far as the Pharisees were concerned, did not deal with hate, holding a grudge, unforgiveness, anger, or revenge—a practice they could indulge in and not break the Law. That is, according to their interpretation of it. The Pharisees could therefore hate, hold a grudge, refuse to forgive, give in to anger or revenge, and not break the sixth command because they did not physically kill anyone. That was all that mattered. They could not envisage an internal righteousness; it was all external. All for show. All for being seen by people so that they could be admired. But Jesus explained that the righteousness of the kingdom of heaven not only had no place for physically murdering somebody but had no place for anger or insult (Matt. 5:22). What is required not to break the sixth commandment in the kingdom of heaven is not showing anger, insult, or hate, but loving your enemies and praying for them.

Jesus later embellished this statement, elaborating on what He meant by being meek in Matthew 5:5.

> You have heard that it was said, "An eye for an eye and a tooth for a tooth." But I say to you, Do not resist the one who is evil. But if anyone slaps you on the right cheek, turn to him the other also....You have heard that it was said, "You shall love your neighbor and hate your enemy." But I say to you, Love your enemies and pray for those who persecute you, so that you may be sons of your Father who is in heaven....For if you love those who love you, what reward do you have?
>
> —MATTHEW 5:38–39, 43–46

This is what is meant by *total forgiveness.* If you forgive your enemies and pray *sincerely* for God to bless them, you are surpassing the righteousness of the Pharisees. The kingdom of heaven, therefore, requires that we love and forgive one another—and *pray for our enemies.* The Holy Spirit would convict us if we did not do these things. A new sense of sin now emerged: grudge holding, unforgiveness, and insulting was murder, according to Jesus. Insulting or holding grudges would not bother the Pharisees.

The truth is, what Jesus teaches is a much higher standard than that of the Mosaic Law. Not only was Jesus against physical murder, but He was upholding a standard that was higher and far more challenging. It is not what gets you to heaven; imputed righteousness does that. But it is what gets you your inheritance—and a reward at the judgment seat of Christ (1 Cor. 3:14; 2 Cor. 5:10).

The seventh command, "You shall not commit adultery" (Exod. 20:14), was interpreted by the Pharisees as do not physically have intercourse with a woman who is not your wife. Under their interpretation of the seventh command, then, lusting or causing one to lust was not sin. They could indulge in lusting—which in modern times would include watching pornography, for example—and feel they had not broken the seventh command. But Jesus said, "I say to you that everyone who looks at a woman with lustful intent has already committed adultery with her in his heart" (Matt. 5:28). You could be a Pharisee and be a slave to pornography without breaking the seventh command. But not in the kingdom of heaven that Jesus came to introduce.

James speaks of our words setting a forest on fire by a spark (Jas. 3:5). This can happen when one asserts an innuendo that has sexual implications—even flattery that is uttered with the intent of causing another to have lustful thoughts. The Pharisee could flirt, flatter, and even touch a woman and not be guilty of breaking the seventh command.

Therefore, Jesus' teaching on the seventh command—like the sixth—demonstrates a much higher and more challenging standard of living than the Law did.

The third command, "You shall not take the name of the LORD your God in vain" (Exod. 20:7), was interpreted by Jesus to refer not merely to swearing—bad language using God's name—but to appealing to God's name to vindicate your point of view, like saying, "I swear by God's Name He is on my side."

A quick way perhaps to understand what Jesus meant is to see how James, His half-brother, applied it. James addressed those poorer Christians who had been disenfranchised by rich, arrogant Christians. (See James 5:1–6.) The poorer Christians felt that God was on their side and against these rich Christians. That was no doubt true. But James cautioned them, "Do not swear" (Jas. 5:12). That is like saying, "Do not say, 'I swear by the name of God, who is on my side and against you, that you will be punished.'"

In other words, these poorer Christians may have

got it right that the richer Christians were in the wrong. But God is no respecter of persons. Even those who had been mistreated were not allowed to show revenge, not to mention bringing in God's name to vindicate themselves. To put it another way, one could be in the right but get it wrong by having a bad attitude. These mistreated Christians must not bring in God's name but quietly let God defend them in His time.

Jesus' interpretation would equally warn people who say "Thus said the Lord" when they prophesy. They are not doing it to make God look good; they are doing it to give themselves credibility and make themselves look good; it is misusing God's name.

The Sermon on the Mount shows a very high standard of living. It can be carried out only by those who have been converted by the Holy Spirit and who are following the Spirit by carrying out Jesus' principles, namely, those who show right living that exceeds the righteousness of the Pharisees.

This is why Jesus said, "You therefore must be perfect, as your heavenly Father is perfect" (Matt. 5:48). That does not mean we can or ever will be sinlessly perfect before we go to heaven. It means that we must mature—an equally accurate word for *teleios*, translated "perfect." We are to be mature, complete, and a finished product in *our* realm on earth as our Father is perfect in *His* realm—heaven.

Three Life Applications

The remaining chapters of the Sermon on the Mount (Matthew chapters 6 and 7) show how Jesus applied His teaching to the lifestyle of Pharisees in three areas.

1. Giving to the poor

The Pharisees, called hypocrites here as Jesus calls them as such several times elsewhere (Matt. 23:1–29), practice their righteousness before other people "in order to be seen by them" (Matt. 6:1). The consequence of doing things to be seen of people: "no reward from your Father who is in heaven," says Jesus. The Pharisees apparently sounded a trumpet in the synagogues and in the streets that they might be "praised by others."

The righteousness that exceeds that of the Pharisees, then, is not to let "your left hand know what your right hand is doing, so that your giving may be in secret" (Matt. 6:3–4). In other words, when we give of our financial means, there is a sense in which we do not even tell ourselves what we give! The good news: "your Father who sees in secret will reward you" (v. 4). We therefore make a choice: Do we want the reward from our Father in heaven or do we want the praise of people? According to Jesus, the Jews missed their Messiah because they made no attempt to receive the praise of God but wanted the praise from one another (John 5:44).

The righteousness that surpasses that of the Pharisees, then, is to give secretly so that the Father in heaven is the only one who knows.

2. Prayer

Jesus tells us not to pray as the hypocrites do: "they love to stand and pray in the synagogues and at the street corners, that they may be seen by others" (Matt. 6:5). Warning: their reward has already been given; they chose being seen by people. Jesus then told us how to pray to be seen of the Father alone: "go to your room and shut the door and pray to your Father who is in secret." He will reward you (v. 6).

This brings up a question: Do we tell people that we pray for them? I have battled with this for years. I think it blesses people to know we pray for them, but is encouraging them our only motive? It is a hard call. John Wesley prayed for two hours each morning, but we would not know this had he not told someone. And yet I am glad to know of Wesley's example! These are the kind of issues we work out with fear and trembling!

3. Fasting

It is noteworthy that Jesus assumes we will fast—go without food. But the principle here is the same as in the two previous examples. We must not let it be known we are fasting—as the hypocrites do: "they disfigure their faces that their fasting may be seen by others" (Matt. 6:16). When we make sure it is known by others that we are fasting—so they will look up to us—we forfeit the reward God would have given.

The righteousness that exceeds that of the Pharisees, then, is giving in secret, praying in secret, and fasting in secret—seeking only the reward that will come from our heavenly Father (Matt. 6:18).

A further embellishment of His treatment of the sixth command came up again in the Sermon on the Mount. First, when Jesus applied one of the reasons for the Lord's Prayer. It is inserted in the Sermon on the Mount in Matthew 6:9–13, but Jesus applies the petition that says, "Forgive us our debts [sins], as we also have forgiven our debtors [those who have sinned against us]" (v. 12). Jesus applies this.

> For if you forgive others their trespasses, your heavenly Father will also forgive you, but if you do not forgive others their trespasses, neither will your Father forgive your trespasses.
> —Matthew 6:14–15

This is not a prayer for salvation; it is addressed to those who are already in the family of God; otherwise they could not call God "Father." Some have objected to praying the Lord's Prayer because it does not end "in Jesus' name." But the name of Jesus is immediately assumed the moment you say, "Our Father." You have no right to call God Father unless you have acknowledged His Son!

The word of Jesus about forfeiting the Father's forgiveness refers not to losing our salvation, which is not possible, but losing *fellowship* with the Father—which is possible, as we saw earlier in 1 John 1:7—walking in the light and having the blood of Jesus cleanse us. Fellowship with the Father is most precious; it is part of coming into our inheritance. We will forfeit this inheritance if we refuse to forgive those who have hurt us in any way.

In Matthew 7:1 Jesus demonstrates yet another application of how the sixth command must be applied, therefore how our righteousness may exceed that of the Pharisees, namely, judging others.

> Judge not, that you be not judged. For with the judgment you pronounce you will be judged, and with the measure you use it will be measured to you. Why do you see the speck in your brother's eye, but do not notice the log that is in your own eye? Or how can you say to your brother, "Let me take the speck out of your eye," when there is the log in your own eye? You hypocrite, first take the log out of your own eye, and then you will see clearly to take the speck out of your brother's eye.
>
> —MATTHEW 7:1–5

This warning about judging others can be traced to Jesus' application of the sixth commandment ("Do not murder") because it reflects anger in one's heart that makes him or her want to judge another. Refusing to judge, then, is a further example of the righteousness that exceeds that of the Pharisees.

You may recall that I said that an important reason for the Sermon on the Mount was to point to the cross. Jesus made what might be called the most stupendous statement He ever made, that He Himself would "fulfill" the Law and the prophets (Matt. 5:17). What a statement! He would do what had never been done, that is, to keep the Law, to fulfill it in every detail. That is why He came; He kept the Law for us. It was the work God sent Him to do—and He intended "to accomplish his [that of the Father] work" (John 4:34). This meant He would live without sinning.

Paul will later say that we are saved not only by Christ's death but also His life (Rom. 5:10). This means that the life of Jesus—His sinlessness and perfect faith—is crucial to His atonement. This meant that Jesus kept the Law for us, was even baptized for us (Matt. 3:13–15), and believed perfectly for us. It was Jesus' own faith as a man that was the efficacious cause of our justification.

This is why our faith is in the faith of Christ! See the King James Version of Romans 3:26 and Galatians 2:16, 20. These verses in the King James Version translate *pistis cristou*—literally, "faith of Christ"—and make complete sense. These show that Jesus' *life* is as important as His *death*.

Did Jesus accomplish the work the Father gave Him? Did He fulfill the Law? Did He do it? YES! That is what Jesus meant when He uttered those words, "It is finished" (John 19:30). Mission accomplished! What is more, *tetelestai*—the Greek translated into "it is finished"—was a colloquial expression in the ancient marketplace that meant "paid in full." Our debt was paid by the life and death of Jesus.

In a word: when Jesus promised to fulfill the Law it was a promise to finish the work the Father sent Him to do.

He did it. Mission accomplished!

Part II:

Reasons You Might Be a Pharisee

CHAPTER 6

Chances Are
You Are a Pharisee

Judge not, that you be not judged. For with the
judgment you pronounce you will be judged, and with
the measure you use it will be measured to you.
Why do you see the speck that is in your brother's eye,
but do not notice the log that is in your own eye?
Or how can you say to your brother, "Let me take the
speck out of your eye," when there is the log in your own
eye? You hypocrite, first take the log out of your own eye,
and then you will see clearly to take the speck out
of your brother's eye.

—Matthew 7:1–5

M

Y FRIEND JACK Taylor once used a phrase
in a sermon, "Chances are you are a Pharisee if…," and I have been intrigued by
the idea ever since. We all need to learn to laugh at
ourselves and not be defensive when our weakness is
touched on. Meekness, a great virtue, could be defined

as the ability to accept a hard criticism without being the slightest bit defensive. The essence of meekness is to be able to accept a criticism—even an insult—without retorting. As John Stott once said, "We are happy to confess before God that we are 'miserable sinners,' but if someone calls us that, we want to punch him in the face!" Yes, I can say it of myself, that I am a great sinner. But I don't want *you* telling me that!

The last time I saw John Stott, by the way, he said to me just before we said good-bye to each other, "If you really knew me, you would spit in my face." A statement like that shows extraordinary humility. I think we could all say that—if we are utterly honest with ourselves. But I don't want someone else to tell me he feels like spitting in my face because he has judged me!

And yet Jesus *did* allow that. They made a crown of thorns and pressed it down on his brow. They put a reed in His right hand as if it were a scepter. "And kneeling before him, they mocked him, saying, 'Hail, King of the Jews!' And they spit on him and took the reed and struck him on the head. And when they had mocked him, they stripped him of the robe and put his own clothes on him and led him away to crucify him" (Matt. 27:29–31). Jesus' response, which Isaiah saw in advance: "He opened not his mouth; like a lamb that is led to the slaughter, and like a sheep that before its shearers is silent, so he opened not his mouth" (Isa. 53:7).

Some who greatly admire the apostle Paul have sometimes been a bit prone to compare him to Jesus in some ways. But never forget that Paul certainly wasn't Jesus and was by no means perfect. As Paul was testifying before the high priest, he said, "I have lived my life before God in all good conscience up to this day" (Acts 23:1). The high priest Ananias was annoyed by Paul's comments and commanded those who stood by him to strike him on the mouth.

Did Paul turn the cheek? No. Did he demonstrate meekness? No. Was he silent? No. Instead, Paul said to Ananias,

> "God is going to strike you, you whitewashed wall! Are you sitting to judge me according to the law, and yet contrary to the law you order me to be struck?"
>
> Those who stood by said, "Would you revile God's high priest?"
>
> And Paul said, "I did not know, brothers, that he was the high priest..."
>
> —Acts 23:3–5

Of course he knew! In any case, he did not display meekness. He wasn't perfect.

A certain measure of meekness is required to work through this chapter because I think it hits all of us. I lead the way, I assure you, in being an expert in being a Pharisee because too much that follows continues to hit me between the eyes. I am not proud of this. But I want you to know I do not see myself as being fully emancipated from this bondage. And yet we are going to look further at the very sins that angered our Lord Jesus most.

These things said, we must never justify ourselves when we see Pharisaism in us. We must admit it and vehemently try not to be this way. We must confess it when we fail. Thank God for good old 1 John 1:9: "If we confess our sins, he is faithful and just to forgive us our sins and to cleanse us from all unrighteousness."

Prayer meetings are the backbone of a good church but can also be the most painfully boring times of the week. This is because there are those who love to hear themselves pray—and drive others mad.

At Westminster Chapel we had regular prayer meetings before the Sunday evening service. Because of one lady who *always* began to pray a minute—sometimes seconds—before 6:10 p.m. when it was time to break up and go into the service (the evening services started at 6:30), I found myself sitting on the edge of my seat in nervous anger. Week after week she would literally start to pray a second or two before I was ready to close the meeting.

I took a little bit of consolation when a deacon said, "Dr. Lloyd-Jones was frustrated with her too. He would say, 'Won't someone quiet that woman?'" But he didn't, I didn't, I'm ashamed to say. Not only that, her prayer was virtually the same week after week. It edified nobody. She loved to hear herself pray. We all knew it. I'm sorry, but I had to go into the evening service so often feeling livid. No one had the nerve to confront her. It is hard to confront Pharisaism.

Paul said, "Brothers, if anyone is caught in any transgression, you who are spiritual should restore him in a spirit of gentleness. Keep watch on yourself, lest you too be tempted" (Gal. 6:1). Yes. I have had to do it many times. That is, as long as it was a clear transgression. Adultery. Theft. Swearing. Lying. It was not easy to do, but restoring such a person like this was a piece of cake compared to dealing with a self-righteous person whose transgression was visible to all but not to him or to her. Oh yes. Dealing with a Pharisaical weakness? I found it almost impossible. A religious spirit is hard to deal with. How do you define a religious spirit? How do you say to someone, "You have a religious spirit"? I found this to be one of the most difficult, delicate matters ever to come up in my ministry over the years.

My British friend Harry Kilbride, who ministered in America and is back home in England, told me of two incidents in one of his former churches in which people had to be lovingly rebuked for their long prayers. In one case, a man would pray the same prayer week after week, and it went on and on: "We praise Thee, O God, for Thy love, Thy sovereignty, Thy omnipotence, this wonderful salvation You have given us in sending Thy Son…" On and on the man would go.

Harry knew that this man kept others from praying and also was in danger of making people run away, especially young people whom he wanted to encourage to come. So he made a public appeal to those who came that perhaps not everybody should pray every single week. The man never came back to the prayer meeting again. It seems he did not care to be truly involved in prayer unless he could pray his long prayers.

The second incident had to do with a lady who prayed much the same way. In this case Dr. Kilbride asked her to see him in the vestry. He asked if she enjoyed the prayer meetings and how she thought they were going. "Oh wonderful, Pastor," she said. He then, as gently as he could—sugarcoating the medicine—asked her if perhaps she might not pray every single week but perhaps once every three weeks, in order to encourage others, especially young people, to pray also. The woman agreed. The problem was, after that, she only came once every three weeks—and she would then pray! She too was not interested in coming unless she prayed.

Jesus said of Pharisees, "They love to stand and pray" (Matt. 6:5), that is, if *people* are listening. Do you think you are spiritual because you "love" to pray? You might be a Pharisee!

These are examples of how Pharisees, though good people in so many ways, are alive and well in the church today. In Westminster Chapel we had a sweet old lady (now in heaven) who prayed aloud every time there was a prayer meeting and would never finish a prayer without condemning those who weren't present. "Lord, You know there are so few of us here. So many don't care to come to a prayer meeting. So many don't love You. They don't want to carry the load. They don't want to intercede." On and on she would go.

It had the effect of making all present *sigh* the moment she began, and we wished she could somehow manage to pray without pointing the finger. It is a subtle form of Pharisaism. It is a religious spirit, as I said, one of the hardest nuts to crack in the church today. It is the enemy of what God wants to do in the here and now.

If, however, Pharisaism makes us angry when we see it in others, we need to see it in ourselves and how it must really grieve the Holy Spirit. Jesus' words perfectly mirrored what the Father wanted said (John 5:19), and we can be equally sure that the Holy Spirit, who is the Spirit of Christ, feels the same things Jesus felt. It is easy to see it in others, but can we see this in ourselves?

This is why I believe this book is important. If certain aspects of the Pharisees raise the holy ire of the Son of God, who was devoid of self-righteousness, I want to be sure I am convicted of Pharisaism in my own heart and life and am doing everything I possibly can *not* to be like the ancient Pharisees of Jesus' day.

What is the possibility that you and I could be Pharisees? What are the signs—or warning signals? Chances are you and I are Pharisees if:

1. We love to point the finger.

It comes easily. And the devil does it best. He is called "the accuser" (Rev. 12:10). You must choose whether you want to play the devil and point the finger or be Jesus, who lets us save face. Jesus actually gives us a selfish motivation for not pointing the finger. "Do not judge, and you will not be judged" (Luke 6:37, NIV). Do you like it when someone points the finger at you? Probably not. According to Jesus, the best way to avoid having someone point the finger at you is that you don't point the finger at them! Do not judge, and you will not be judged!

I will forfeit the benefit of the promise that I won't be judged if I play the role of the accuser. On the other hand, if I choose the pointing of the finger rather than let God sort out the person I want to condemn, I too "will be judged" (Matt. 7:1). Believe me, I know this to be true even by experience! It is safer and far better to cease pointing the finger ever again. You will never be sorry. As a rule of thumb, ask yourself if what you are thinking to say will meet another's *need*. Put these questions to yourself before you speak:

N—is it *necessary* to say this?

E—will it *emancipate*—help set the person free?

E—will it *energize*—will it excite or edify?

D—will it *dignify* the person?

In Isaiah 58 we have the account of ancient Jews who fasted and prayed with apparently getting no benefit from it. They prayed, "Why have we fasted, and you see it not? Why have we humbled ourselves, and you take no knowledge of it?" (Isa. 58:3). Isaiah suggests a different kind of fast: "to share your bread with the hungry and bring the homeless poor into your house" (v. 7).

Their problem was that they enjoyed fasting. "In the day of your fast you seek your own pleasure, and oppress all your workers. Behold, you fast only to quarrel and to fight and to hit with a wicked fast. Fasting like yours this day will not make your voice to be heard on high" (vv. 3–4). The prophet then tells them the kind of fast that will get God's attention. I won't repeat all that was said here, but I want to call attention to one phrase; among the various things that Isaiah tells them they must get rid of is "the pointing of the finger" (v. 9).

What a picturesque phrase! It sums up judging another person who you think needs sorting out. It is *personal* pointing of the finger. This person gets your goat. This does not refer to upholding objective truth of the gospel but to personal relationships. It comes close to the principles laid down in Dale Carnegie's *How to Win Friends and Influence People*, which I mentioned earlier. It's not a Christian book but it unwittingly upholds some of Jesus' practical teaching, such as letting the other person save face.

I have not fasted a lot in my lifetime, but I have a few times—especially when we as a church would have days of prayer and fasting. It is my experience that not a lot usually happens when one fasts. During a holiday in Florida many years ago, when I was in the deepest crisis of my entire ministry, I fasted several days—taking in only liquids. During that time I felt singularly *nothing*. But the benefit was enjoyed later.

What I have also discovered is that I am not always in a spiritual "mood" during a time I'm fasting. For one thing, I'm hungry. I have also experienced times—I am ashamed to say—I was in an irritable mood. I found myself pointing the finger at Louise! Imagine that! Trying to fast—the purpose of which is mainly to get God's attention—and pointing the finger!

That is exactly what the ancient Israelites did. And God refused to affirm their fast. It does, therefore, suggest that if we fast, we should be clear that our lives are otherwise pleasing to the Lord. We must never—ever—think that one form of righteousness—fasting—compensates for a gross deficiency in our lives like pointing the finger!

Pointing the finger refers to judging another when it is *personal.* You must never point the finger when your feeling is personal, such as someone irritating you, hurting you, speaking evil of you, or wanting to make you look bad. In such a case, you are not allowed to retort or respond at all. This is when meekness must be fully displayed, even if the temptation to defend yourself is severe. Never forget: vengeance belongs to the Lord (Rom. 12:19).

What if it's not personal?

Is it OK to point the finger if the matter is not personal? Perhaps. But be careful. There can be a thin line between upholding the integrity of Scripture—which one must do—and trying to sort out a person's doctrine. If someone is propagating error and you are not personally involved, there may be room for speaking out.

Question: When does one have a duty to speak up? Answer: when your ego is not involved but you are objectively upholding the truth, you may speak out. But even here one must be extremely careful or he or she will grieve the Holy Spirit. One must speak lovingly and without any bitterness (Eph. 4:30–32).

Paul said that in the last days there will be those people who "will not endure sound teaching, but having itching ears will accumulate for themselves teachers to suit their own passions and will turn away from listening to the truth" (2 Tim. 4:3–4). When it is clear that people only follow a minister for a "feel good" result and are not interested in objective truth and repenting from sin, yes, something needs to be said. But one must be sure that there is no personal ego involved, that there is no jealousy, and that one is truly broken. Because Satan is pleased with a ministry that does not uphold Holy Scripture and the gospel. Remember, ask if what you are tempted to say will meet a NEED.

Only Jesus was sinlessly perfect. He is qualified to point the finger because it is never selfish; it is never to embarrass or make a person feel insignificant. What is more, all He ever said mirrored the will of the Father; He only said and did what the Father told Him to do (John 5:19).

But if you love to point the finger, chances are you are a Pharisee.

Chances are you and I are Pharisees if:

2. We love to say "Gotcha!"

We love to catch the person in the act whereby they cannot deny that they got caught. The Pharisees did exactly that one day. They brought a woman to Jesus who had been caught in adultery. They said, "Teacher, this woman has been caught in the act of adultery. Now in the Law, Moses commanded us to stone such women. So what do you say?" (John 8:4–5). They were playing the "gotcha" game with Jesus. John records that they said this "to test him, that they might have some charge to bring against him" (v. 6).

Jesus stooped over and wrote with His finger in the dirt. There have been guesses as to what He wrote. Did He just scribble in the ground? Did He write the names of those Pharisees who brought the woman to show that He knew what was in each man's heart? Did He write the names of women that the Pharisees would recognize that they themselves had been with?

All we know is, He stood up and said to them, "Let him who is without sin among you be the first to throw a stone at her" (v. 7). He then continued to write in the ground. What followed? "They went away one by one, beginning with the older ones, and Jesus was left alone with the woman standing before him" (v. 9). Then Jesus stood up and said to her, "Woman, where are they? Has no one condemned you?" (v. 10). She said, "No one, Lord." Then came a wonderful example of grace: "Neither do I condemn you; go, and from now on sin no more" (v. 11).

Many readers will know John 3:16: "For God so loved the world, that he gave his only Son, that whoever believes in him should not perish but have eternal life." Martin Luther is often quoted as saying that John 3:16 is the gospel in a nutshell. But how many of us know the next verse—John 3:17: "For God did not send his Son into the world to condemn the world, but in order that the world might be saved through him"?

Hence Jesus said to the woman found in the act of adultery: "Neither do I condemn you." It was no doubt the sweetest news this woman ever heard. And yet the first work of the Holy Spirit is to convict of sin—not because we are condemned but that we might see our own sin, to be convicted of it so we will live a life that is honoring to God. Therefore Jesus added to this woman, "Go, and from now on sin no more."

The world loves to play the "Gotcha" game with God and His Word. They love to find verses that seem to contradict each other so that they can satisfy themselves they do not have to believe the Bible anymore. People do this when they don't want to believe a particular doctrine—like creation for example (Gen. 1:27); they look for holes in the teaching so they can rid themselves of any guilt for not believing in that teaching—whether it be the truth of the gospel, creation *ex nihilo* [out of nothing], the infallibility of Scripture, salvation by grace alone, or for the view that the gifts of the Spirit did not cease with the first century of Christianity. Some "cessationists" (those who believe God does not perform miracles nowadays) even rejoice when a person is not healed.

If you love playing "gotcha" with people who differ with you theologically so you clearly can point out their weaknesses, you just might be a Pharisee!

It is said that a journalist's dream is to write an article or book in order to say, "Gotcha!"—like finding someone highly respected, such as Billy Graham or Mother Teresa, and exposing their imperfections.

At a presidential press conference a journalist often asks "Gotcha" questions, hoping to embarrass the president. If he or she succeeds, he or she might get him or her own book published—or he or she might become famous.

God knows we all have skeletons in the cupboard, and if God decided to tell the world what He knows about each of us, we would die on the spot. But there is a better way to live.

Joseph, the favorite son of Jacob, fanaticized that he would see his dreams fulfilled—namely that of his brothers bowing down to him (Gen. 37:6–9). They had wickedly decided to get rid of him, but finally let him live. Joseph thought that God gave him those dreams so that one day he could say, "Gotcha!" to them. The day came. The dreams were perfectly fulfilled. But God had other plans. God delayed the fulfillment of these dreams so that Joseph was a different man. So when the dreams were actually fulfilled, Joseph was a changed man, and instead of looking at them with glee in their helpless state, he wept over them and totally forgave them (Gen. 45:1–11). That was the secret of his greatness and the reason God trusted him with such a lofty status.

Are you waiting to say "Gotcha!" to someone who has maligned you? Are you waiting to say "Gotcha!" to someone whose doctrine you want to expose? Caution: you just might be a Pharisee.

You might also find out that God has a surprising plan for you.

Chances are you and I are Pharisees if:

3. We are good at sending people on a guilt trip.

The Pharisees tried to do a "Gotcha!" again and again over the way Jesus performed miracles on the Sabbath and allowed things to be done on the Sabbath that seemed to go against the Law. When His disciples were hungry on the Sabbath and plucked heads of grain and began to eat, the Pharisees seized the moment to condemn both Jesus and His disciples.

The Pharisees might have succeeded in making Jesus' disciples feel guilty over this, but Jesus defended them. He did so by referring to Scripture. "Have you not read what David did when he was hungry?" Jesus asked. He referred to the occasion when David was hungry and entered the house of God and ate the bread of the Presence "which was not lawful," which was for the priests. He then put this question to the Pharisees and then made a stupendous claim for Himself.

> Or have you not read in the Law how on the Sabbath the priests in the temple profane the Sabbath and are guiltless? I tell you, something greater than the temple is here. And if you had known what this means, "I desire mercy, and not sacrifice," you would not have condemned the guiltless. For the Son of Man is lord of the Sabbath.
>
> —MATTHEW 12:5–8

The Law invariably finds people guilty. When you have interpretations of the Law that exceed the Law—or rules of your own you think are valid—it only widens the scope for the possibility of guilt. And when we superimpose our rules and wishes on friends or enemies in order to require that they come up to our standard, we become Pharisees.

You may recall that the Pharisees had built fences that surrounded the Law—rules not in the Law. But they reckoned if they did not cross over the line with their fences, they would most certainly not break the Law. This is what is meant by their "traditions." They wanted people to feel guilty if the people did not uphold their traditions. Their traditions were not rooted in Scripture but gave them a way to justify what they wanted to believe. Jesus said, "For the sake of your tradition you have made void the word of God" (Matt. 15:6). Then, quoting Isaiah 29:13, He said,

> This people honors me with their lips, but their heart is far from me; in vain do they worship me, teaching as doctrines the commandments of men.
>
> —MATTHEW 15:8–9

As I mentioned earlier, the Pharisees also criticized Jesus for not washing before the meal. This was not a Scriptural requirement but another of their traditions. It had nothing to do with hygiene; it was all liturgy and tradition. A Pharisee had invited Jesus to dine with him but was astonished to see that Jesus did not first wash before dinner. Jesus knew what was in the Pharisee's heart and said to him, "Now you Pharisees cleanse the outside of the cup and of the dish, but inside you are full of greed and wickedness. You fools! Did not he who made the outside make the inside also?" (Luke 11:39–40).

The Pharisees came up with extra-biblical ways to make people feel guilty. God is not like that. The gospel summed up: we are justified by faith in Christ alone and are to walk by faith, not by a book of rules. God does not want any of us to feel guilty. On the contrary, He gives the Holy Spirit whereby we say to Him, *"Abba"* Father (Rom. 8:15). That means intimacy with the Lord by the Holy Spirit. When the guilt is gone and we have fellowship with the Father, the joy is greater than any this world can offer.

It proves we have totally forgiven someone when we will not let them feel guilty. We see this in the way Joseph treated his guilty brothers when they were found out. He said to them, "Do not be distressed or angry with yourselves" (Gen. 45:5). Have you ever said to someone, "I forgive you," but as you do, you hope they will feel bad about it? It takes minimal grace to forgive someone who is sorry for what they did to you. Would you like to know how to get a great victory? Forgive them when they are not sorry! Forgive them if they don't even know what they did wrong!

What often gets our goat is that those who have hurt us don't know how deeply hurt we are. We want somehow to let them know how hurt we are. I do understand! But here is the secret to getting a major victory: pray for them to be blessed when they are not sorry for what they did. Pray for them when they don't even realize what they did.

God knows. Get your victory from an audience of One—God only. Total forgiveness therefore means we do not send another person on a guilt trip; we are aware of what *we* have been forgiven of, and we must therefore treat others as God has treated us.

Are you good at giving a person a guilt trip? Do you like making people feel guilty? Chances are that you might be a Pharisee.

Chances are you and I are Pharisees if:

4. We require people to live up to standards not written in Scripture.

Do you require duties of others that you yourself do not do? Caution: you just might be a Pharisee.

The Pharisees, said Jesus, "tie up heavy burdens, hard to bear, and lay them on people's shoulders, but they themselves are not willing to move them with their finger" (Matt. 23:4). It is somewhat like preachers who tell their congregations to witness for Jesus in the streets and in the workplace, but they themselves never mention the gospel except when they are in the pulpit.

I grew up in a church in which they often spoke of standards—supposedly "godly" standards. As I said earlier, I could not go to the movies as a child. My mother did not wear lipstick or makeup. My father would not read a Sunday newspaper, nor could I. Never mind that the Sunday newspapers were printed on Saturdays and the Monday morning newspapers—which he read—were printed on Sundays. I could not play basketball in my own backyard on Sunday.

Some preachers in my old denomination seemed to try to outdo each other on how strict you could be. One preacher spoke against a man wearing a handkerchief in a lapel pocket! I will repeat: I always felt sorry for the teenage girls in my church because they were the only ones in their school who could not wear makeup. When we impose rules on people that are not solidly written in the Word of God—even though we might justify them for some reason or another—we risk being the Pharisees of our day. It only adds to people's bondage.

I urged members of Westminster Chapel to pray thirty minutes a day, but it was never a requirement. It was not a rule, only a suggestion. But standards are rules that people must live by or be "out" rather than "in." God does not like this. Pharisees do.

Three Jewish Traditions

I will mention three traditions that most modern orthodox Jews practice.

First, orthodox Jews—certainly when they pray at the Western Wall in Jerusalem—will not pronounce the name of the Lord, *Yahweh.* When they come to *Yahweh* in Scripture, or when they pray, they will not utter *"Yahweh"* but only *Adonai,* also meaning Lord. There is something lovely and special about this; they want to show reverence and honor to the name of God. That said, I asked Sir Rabbi David Rosen if this is taught anywhere in Scripture. He said there is nothing in the Bible that requires this. There is nothing wrong with praying like this or reading the Scripture and not uttering *Yahweh*; but it is a choice nearly all Jews consciously make. As I said, they do it to honor the name of the Lord.

Second, the use of phylacteries. I never understood

this until I saw an orthodox Jewish man on a flight to Tel Aviv stand up in the aisle and put his phylactery on and take it off. It was no doubt important to him that he did this before all the passengers. Jesus, when bringing up the subject of phylacteries, said that Pharisees do everything for people to see (Matt. 23:5). Phylacteries are leather straps that connect to a small black leather box in which are inscribed scriptures. They are worn on the left wrist and used in morning prayers. This Jewish man on the plane had a routine that I did not grasp, although he did not take long— perhaps five or ten minutes at the most. Jesus actually made fun of this, which shows it is ancient tradition. It borders on superstition. "They make their phylacteries broad and their fringes [borders on their garments] long" (Matt. 23:5).

Third, orthodox women's hair. Orthodox Jewish women will not let their hair be seen. They either wear clothing that completely covers their own hair or wear a wig so that you cannot see their hair. Again, this is a tradition; there is nothing in the Bible that says a woman should not let her hair show.

You may recall that my own mother wore her hair long, usually in a bun. Paul talks about a woman's "glory" being her hair (1 Cor. 11:15). There is a Christian tradition, however, that says that a woman must have a "covering"—e.g., a hat or scarf—in church. Others argue that long hair is covering enough. In the early

days of my ministry at Westminster Chapel most of
the ladies wore hats. I received an anonymous letter
stating that Louise was holding up revival because
she did not wear a hat! Oh well. As Yogi Berra said,
"Never answer an anonymous letter!"

Do you have a tradition—or rules not in Scripture—
you believe people should live by? Caution: you just
might be a Pharisee.

Chances are you and I are Pharisees if:

5. We practice guilt by association.

I fear I have done this too many times. I'll give you
a recent example. A man whose ministry has blessed
me over the years has recently become associated with
a ministry that has gone very liberal. He no longer
wants to be known as an Evangelical. I was sobered to
discover this; does this mean the man and the liberal
ministry are now of the same ilk? Should I let this sort
of thing bother me? I keep hoping it's not true. That
said, I too have no doubt disappointed some people
because of places I have preached and friendships I
have had.

I was photographed with Bishop Desmond Tutu a
few years ago. He had contributed one of his prayers—
a wonderful prayer—to Louise's book *Great Christian
Prayers*. I was in Cape Town and felt flattered that he
was quite willing to meet with me. I wanted to thank
him for his amazing prayer. I showed a friend the
photo that I was going to put on Twitter. My friend

simply noted that Bishop Tutu had championed same-sex marriage—even before it became accepted as it is today. I did not know this and was glad to be spared of inevitable criticism. But should I have let the photo be on my Twitter anyway—and not care what people think? Or would this hurt some people who might think I am at one with Tutu? I decided I did not want needlessly to offend people and omitted using it. Sometimes a person is not necessarily Pharisaical who warns us about our apparent associations.

Guilt by association like the ancient Pharisees practiced is when we accuse people of being unclean, unrighteous, or out of order when they mix with people of other faiths, varying views, or questionable lifestyles. If I accept an invitation to preach to a group with whom I do not agree theologically, does it make me guilty of condoning what they believe? No. But some would accuse me. Pharisees would. Not Jesus. If I invite a person to preach for me who happens to hold to views I am uncomfortable with, does this make me guilty by having this person in my pulpit? No. If I pray with a fellow Christian who is not totally at one with me doctrinally, does that make me guilty by associating with them in this way? No.

But if I accuse you of being wicked because you are having a meal with a sinner, then I am a Pharisee. If I try to make you feel shameful because you choose to spend time with a person I don't agree with, I am a Pharisee.

The Pharisees leveled this charge at Jesus. Tax collectors and sinners were all drawing near to hear Jesus. The Pharisees grumbled, saying, "This man receives sinners and eats with them" (Luke 15:2). For the Pharisees that was convincing evidence that Jesus should be condemned. They were looking for such an opportunity. They did not know how to handle His miracles, His way of applying Scripture, or His arguments. But when they noticed that His company was made up of tax collectors and "sinners," that was the evidence they were looking for!

Billy Graham was sometimes accused of great compromise for having certain people on the platform with him—some of whom were outspoken ecumenists and theological liberals. This to some justified their rejection of Billy Graham. Billy's reply was that these people need *Him*! Jesus' reply concerning his association with tax collectors was virtually the same: they need Him! Indeed, "Those who are well have no need of a physician, but those who are sick" (Matt. 9:12). Then Jesus added, "Go and learn what this means, 'I desire mercy, and not sacrifice.' For I came not to call the righteous, but sinners" (v. 13).

Shortly after retiring to America, I received an invitation to speak at a Catholic conference in Minnesota. My immediate thought, I am ashamed to admit, was worrying what people would say about me if this word got out. A group of Catholics had heard me speak at a Lutheran church in St. Paul; they were apparently blessed by my messages. I knew I should go speak for them, although I had not spoken for Catholics before. I agreed to go.

I was met by a man who had a statue of the Virgin Mary on the dashboard of his car. I felt a bit strange, having been critical of people who did this sort of thing. But the conversation with the man convinced me he was not only a Christian but a very committed one. I was amazed. I didn't expect this. In minutes I felt at home with him as I did with godly people I knew well.

As for preaching for these people in the Minneapolis diocese, they responded to my preaching on total forgiveness and the sensitivity of the Spirit with the same earnestness as almost anybody I had addressed in the world. I felt ashamed that I had these thoughts, not to mention being concerned that I feared what people would say about me. Shame on me! I later remembered that Dr. Martyn Lloyd-Jones used to say he would preach for the pope if invited, although it would not mean he would have the pope preach for him!

I have also observed that wherever I preached total forgiveness throughout the world, the most committed Christians—so it seemed—were the first to stand up to forgive others. This has been universal, that the more lively and faithful Christians were always the first to stand up to forgive! I say this based on pastors' observations that their most faithful members were quick to stand while those who were irregular in attendance and involvement or rarely come to church usually did not stand or come forward. I say this because those Catholic Christians were as eager to stand up and forgive as much as any lively church I have ever addressed.

What was equally interesting was that near the same time I was invited to preach in a prominent historic church in southeast Georgia. I preached the exact same message on total forgiveness. The lowest number I can *ever* recall stood! It taught me a lesson. And yet I admit to showing my own Pharisaism by making a judgment on how many stand for forgiveness as opposed to those who don't. See there, I am a Pharisee.

Most of my friends in the United States are very much for Israel. A lot of my friends in Britain are pro-Palestinian. I have always had a soft spot for Israel, but when I was invited to meet Yasser Arafat and Palestinian leaders and hear their story, I realized I had been not only biased but had not remotely considered those Palestinian Christians for whom almost nobody in America (I fear) had prayed. As I said above, I offended a number of my fellow Christians in America who felt I betrayed Israel by my association with Arafat and praying for some Palestinian leaders. In much the same way Jesus offended Jews by His show of respect for Samaritans (Luke 10:33; John 4:7–42).

It is times and occasions like these that we must remember we are being watched by One who writes things down in heaven (Mal. 3:16). Our decisions, performance, and behavior are for an audience of One. Otherwise we make the same fatal error of the Pharisees who could not believe in their promised Messiah because they were more concerned about what people thought than what God thought (John 5:44).

These things said, I am a robust Protestant; Martin Luther—who wasn't perfect—is one of my heroes. Furthermore, I truly do love Muslims and Palestinians. And I also await the blindness on Israel to be lifted in these last days. It is hard to say which will come first: massive conversions of Muslims to Jesus Christ, which might provoke Israel to jealousy (Rom. 11:11), or the blindness on Israel lifted, which will result in millions of Jews being saved.

Chances are you and I are Pharisees if:

6. We assume something or someone is of the devil when their ministry makes us uncomfortable.

The Pharisees could not deny that Jesus performed miracles. If they said that these miracles were done by God, it would have condoned Jesus' behavior and put themselves to shame. So they resorted to a trick that has been repeated many times since: they attributed what was done to the devil. In this, even Martin Luther became a Pharisee. He reportedly once said of his rival, Ulrich Zwingli (1484–1531), "Zwingli's God is my devil," because of differing views regarding the Lord's Supper. What a horrible thing to say! If you and I are threatened by someone's success and notice how popular they are but have no answer except to say, "They are of the devil," we are Pharisees.

It is fair to say that a certain person or people may be "misguided" or are in "theological error" if we oppose them. But to claim they are of the devil is dangerous stuff. Indeed, the comment by the people, "He [Jesus] has an unclean spirit" (Mark 3:30), is what led to Jesus' teaching regarding the blasphemy of the Holy Spirit: "Whoever blasphemes against the Holy Spirit never has forgiveness, but is guilty of an eternal sin" (v. 29).

If you or I ever say someone is of the devil or is demon-possessed, we had better be right. The Pharisees said this about Jesus. Not all of them said this of course; Nicodemus was a Pharisee and became a faithful follower of Jesus (John 19:39). Saul of Tarsus was a Pharisee (Acts 26:5; Phil. 3:5). But most denied Jesus and led the way in His crucifixion. You and I are modern Pharisees if we resort to the ultimate putdown—"they are of the devil"—in order to make our opponents look bad. Jesus would not do that.

I know of people who say that speaking in tongues

is of the devil. It could be. Satan is a great coun-
terfeiter. One of my earliest mentors believed that
speaking in tongues is of the devil. It made me biased
against Pentecostals and Charismatics for years. Then
one day—unexpectedly as I was in prayer—I spoke
in tongues! I thank God that He overruled and gave
me this gift. I pray in tongues every day. Some of my
best friends lament my saying this. Why should I be
ashamed of this? Paul wasn't (1 Cor. 14:18). I am honored that God would bestow this gift, especially when
I wasn't remotely thinking of such a thing!

Chances are you and I are Pharisees if:

7. We say a person is not a Christian if they disagree with us.

We say they are not saved or have not been converted if they oppose us. This is judging just like the
Pharisees did. It is a quick cop-out; it is our way of
punishing the person with whom we disagree. Instead
of saying politely that they for some reason disagree
with us, we glibly say, "These people aren't even saved."

There is always the possibility in some cases, of
course, that those who attack us are not truly converted. But why say that? Why not give them the benefit of the doubt? Why resort to the ultimate insult
just because they don't agree with us? It is almost
childish to label a person an unbeliever just because
we don't agree.

Even if they are unsaved, if we treat them with love

and dignity, they may be converted one day and will love and respect us for the way we treated them in the meantime. A good rule of thumb: when you fall out with a person, treat them with such dignity that they will respect you when you make up. Pharisees don't want to make up with people.

I realize that some of these observations slightly overlap. But judging people was what the Pharisees were best at and possibly what they were best known for. For example, Jesus cast a demon out of a man who was deaf-mute. When the man spoke, the crowds were amazed and said that nothing like this had been seen in Israel before. But the Pharisees accused Jesus of casting out demons by the prince of demons—Beelzebub (Matt. 9:32–34; 12:24).

A common ploy of some, then, is to dismiss their critics by saying, "These people have never been converted." Some of us who are reformed in theology are sadly prime examples of what I am discussing in this section. A prominent London minister said of the founder of a Bible college, "I doubt the man was ever converted," because they differed on the place of the Law in the Christian life.

And when certain people opposed my ministry at Westminster Chapel, some refused to affirm that I was a Christian. Indeed, I too was tempted to say of some of my fiercest critics, "These people are not saved." But although the battle was heated in those days, I was mercifully kept from saying such things. The truth is, I do believe, all my opponents were truly converted people. The best of people disagree. How wrong it was of Martin Luther to say of Zwingli, a very godly man: "Zwingli's God is my devil."

Some have made the observation that there are two kinds of Scotsmen: those who love to hear the gospel preached and those who only go to church to see if the gospel was preached! I have been guilty of being like this too, I have to admit. But I am playing the Pharisee when I do this.

Chances are you and I are Pharisees if:

8. We esteem "the way we've always done it" above change, even when the latter is not heretical.

Remember that the Pharisees made the Word of God of no effect by their traditions (Matt. 15:6). Their own traditions were not based on Scripture but their peculiar rules. When new ways of doing things that are not contrary to Scripture emerge, you and I must beware of falling into the trap of always wanting the "old wine." Those who say, "The old is good" (Luke 5:39), want to stay in their comfort zone—to keep the taste they are used to. All new movements God raises up require change. Every person described in Hebrews 11 had to move out of their comfort zones. They all broke with tradition.

At Westminster Chapel I had a fight on my hands because I asked the organist to play songs like "Turn

Your Eyes Upon Jesus" or "He Is Lord" as a prelude rather than Mozart and Chopin. The latter, I was told, made our revered Willis pipe organ sound better. Some even said it was more conducive to worship! In other words, the organist playing Mozart or Chopin— as long as it was classical music, some said—enabled one to feel the presence of God!

I myself was torn within over this. I happen to love Mozart and Chopin. I love the music of Rachmaninoff. I even used to ask my organist to play Saint Saens' *Organ Symphony* after the service. I happen to love the sound of a pipe organ. We were told that our organ was one of the top three best pipe organs in London. I doubt this, but I truly loved our Willis pipe organ.

But when the Holy Spirit began to move in the Chapel, especially following the visit by Arthur Blessitt, it was clear to me that we should leave Chopin to one side and ask the organist to play modern choruses, most of which were directly quoting Scripture. I am ashamed to admit it, but when Arthur said to me, "Don't you have someone who plays a guitar," I resented it at first. I was way outside my comfort zone when we began singing contemporary music to a guitar.

My old friend Jon Bush used to say that the last seven words of a dying church are "We never did it that way before."

Chances are you and I are Pharisees if:

9. We do not practice what we preach.

Jesus plainly said of Pharisees that they "do not practice what they preach" (Matt. 23:3). I cannot think of a greater hypocrisy on the planet than demanding of another person what I would not do myself. I myself bordered on being like this. I would tell my people to go out and witness for Christ, but I felt I had done my duty by preaching from a pulpit. But when Arthur Blessitt said to me during the second week he was with us, "We need to get out in the streets," I died a thousand deaths. It was a vision a week or so later I had one Friday evening in May 1982 that drove me to talking to passersby in Buckingham Gate. It led to our Pilot Light ministry. It is easier to preach to thousands than it is to talk to one person—especially if they are total strangers.

Someone said to Arthur, "How is it that God speaks to you so clearly but doesn't speak that way to me?" Arthur replied: "Have you ever had an inner feeling you should witness to a person you didn't know about Jesus?" The person replied, "As a matter of fact I have." Arthur then said: "Start obeying that voice and it will become clearer and clearer."

This is true. Paul said we should share our faith to "be effective in deepening your understanding of every good thing we share for the sake of Christ" (Philem. 6, NIV). Not only a better understanding but a closer walk with the Holy Spirit, which may truly result in hearing Him speak. "As the Holy Spirit says, 'Today, if you hear his voice'" (Heb. 3:7). I can testify that hearing from God has become far more real to me since I began talking to people I had not met about Jesus—whether on the streets, on a plane, or in a taxi.

What turned Mahatma Gandhi against Christianity was Christians. When I first preached in Durban, South Africa—where Gandhi first came into contact with Christians—I was soberly reminded of this. I also came into contact with some of the high Calvinists in the Reformed church in South Africa. It is believed by some that Gandhi said: "I like your Christ. I do not like your Christians. Your Christians are so unlike your Christ." I am sorry to say that it was people of this theological ilk of whom Gandhi was speaking.

The greatest testimony we give to the world is not our articulate theology or eloquent way of presenting it but their discovery that we are *real*—that we really do practice what we preach. This does not mean we are perfect or never sin. "If we claim to be without sin, we deceive ourselves and the truth is not in us" (1 John 1:8). But if our faces, hearts, and lives reflect the love of Jesus, people are going to want what we've got. As a Muslim businessman said to Arthur Blessitt in a bar in Jordan, "I want what you've got"—referring to Arthur's countenance.

> 'Twas not the truth you taught,
>> to you so clear, to me so dim,

135

But when you came to me,
    you brought a sense of Him.
And from your eyes He beckons me,
    and from your lips His love was shed,
Till I lose sight of you
    and see the Christ instead.[1]

—Beatrice Cleland

Chances are you and I are Pharisees if:

10. We are more comfortable talking about the mighty movements of God of yesterday than today.

Jesus spent more time elaborating on this than all the other points He made. I myself have been deeply gripped by His statement here. I am sure this is partly because of the way we were criticized for having Arthur Blessitt. Arthur often reminded me of certain biblical characters. One magazine that had an article in it criticizing him included another article in the same issue praising George Whitefield. The fact is that George Whitefield would do outrageous things that, if done today, would be severely criticized. But because Whitefield lived two hundred years ago and was reformed in his theology, his methods were overlooked. Jesus put it like this.

> Woe to you, scribes and Pharisees, hypocrites! For you build the tombs of the prophets and decorate the monuments of the righteous, saying, "If we had lived in the days of our

fathers, we would not have taken part with
them in shedding the blood of the prophets."
Thus you witness against yourselves that you
are sons of those who murdered the prophets.
Fill up, then, the measure of your fathers. You
serpents, you brood of vipers, how are you to
escape being sentenced to hell? Therefore I send
you prophets and wise men and scribes, some
of whom you will kill and crucify, and some
of whom you will flog in your synagogues and
persecute from town to town, so that on you
may come all the righteous blood shed on earth,
from the blood of righteous Abel to the blood
of Zechariah the son of Barachiah, whom you
murdered between the sanctuary and the altar.
Truly, I say to you, all these things will come
upon this generation.

—MATTHEW 23:29–36

The Pharisees thought themselves pious and faithful
because they decorated the tombs of the prophets. The
Pharisees even fancied that they would have recognized God at work and would not have been critical
of what God was doing had they been around in previous generations. It is like saying we would not have
crucified Jesus had we been around at that time. This
is sheer self-righteousness. We all crucified Jesus. We
all are critical of what God is up to in the here and
now—it always means going outside our comfort
zone—unless He opens our eyes. It is also wrong to

dismiss what is happening today because it does not repeat what has happened before. There was no clear precedent that I know of for what characterized the Welsh Revival—almost no preaching but all singing. In any case, God does not always do the same thing twice. We must be willing to lose face for God's glory and recognize that God may be working right before our eyes. The offense is to say this is God at work *now*.

This very issue—that God is *now* at work—is what initially offended Jesus' hearers when He read from Isaiah 61:1 as I mentioned earlier.

> The Spirit of the Lord is upon me, because he has anointed me to proclaim good news to the poor. He has sent me to proclaim liberty to the captives and recovering of sight to the blind, to set at liberty those who are oppressed, to proclaim the year of the Lord's favor.
>
> —Luke 4:18–19

So far, so good. That is, until the Lord Jesus rolled up the scroll and said, "*Today* this Scripture has been fulfilled in your hearing" (Luke 4:21, emphasis added). After that, all hell broke loose and the people turned on Jesus and tried to kill Him (Luke 4:22–30). Had Jesus said, "This *will* be fulfilled in the future," no one would have been upset. Or had He said that this promise referred to a previous generation, no one would have criticized. Or if He said nothing at all!

The offense was to claim that God is at work power-fully now—and in an unprecedented way.

Chances are you and I are Pharisees if:

11. We take ourselves too seriously.

Don't we all? But the Pharisees felt they were God's remnant and that it was up to them alone to preserve the Law by their traditions. They took themselves very seriously by the attention they demanded, the way they dressed, the way they tried to trap Jesus, demanding to be called "Rabbi" and insisting on seats of honor. This is the lifestyle of a Pharisee, and it is not a good sign at all when we take ourselves very seriously.

This means we can't laugh at ourselves—certainly we can't cope with being laughed at, we can't listen to criticism without being defensive or be passed by without sulking when we thought we should be invited. The most secure people are those who can laugh at themselves, accept criticism without being defensive, and be passed over when they think they should have been consulted or invited. The main psychological problem of the Pharisees was they were insecure. They are like some of us who won't introduce ourselves to someone we haven't met; we wait to be introduced or the person will not show us a lot of respect!

There is an old British joke that helps people to see some of the possible differences between an Englishman, a Welshman, a Scotsman, and an Irishman.

> Two Englishmen, two Welshmen, two
> Scotsmen, and two Irishmen were marooned
> on a small uninhabited island in the South
> Pacific—but were discovered two years later.
> The two Scotsmen had formed a bank and
> were trading shells with each other. The two
> Welshmen had formed a choir and were singing.
> The two Irishmen had killed each other off in
> a fight. The two Englishmen were waiting to
> be introduced.

In this way I am a bit like an Englishman. I want
to get off to a good start with someone I have heard
a lot about. It's easier on my ego when I am introduced to him or her; I might appear unimportant if
I introduce myself! I will never forget how I first met
Graham Kendrick. He walked up to me to thank me
for a sermon he had heard me preach, not telling me
who he was. I thanked him and said, "Who are you?"
He told me his name. I am ashamed to say I had never
heard of him. This was when I rarely preached outside
Westminster Chapel. I found out he had written the
hymn "Restore, O Lord"[2] and many others. Indeed,
he is the greatest hymn writer since Charles Wesley.
Another person of that stature—certainly one who
takes himself very seriously—would possibly never
come up to me like that.

While I am name-dropping, I will tell how I met
Matt Redman, also one of the greatest songwriters

of our generation. I was at J. John's Evangelistic Conference two years ago. Matt and I were walking in opposite directions, but he said, "Hi, R. T." I did not recognize him and barely nodded. Several minutes later J. John publicly recognized Matt. I turned and realized that he was the one who kindly spoke to me. I walked over to him immediately and said, "I am so embarrassed that I didn't know who you were." The result of this has been that we have become very close friends.

Both Graham and Matt are Englishmen, but happily they don't take themselves seriously and wait to be introduced!

Chances are you and I are Pharisees if:

12. We judge by outward appearance.

"Do not judge by appearance," Jesus said to the Pharisees (John 7:24). Samuel, the great prophet of the Old Testament, had to learn this lesson—as we all do in some way. The Lord said to him as he was trying to discern who would be the next king, "Do not look on his appearance or on the height of his stature...For the LORD sees not as man sees: man looks on the outward appearance, but the LORD looks on the heart" (1 Sam. 16:7).

This section borders on guilt by association but is slightly different. I refer to when we don't like the way a person dresses—too fashionable, too expensive, or too casual; we don't like their accent—too posh or too working class; we don't approve of their education or lack of it or where they received it; we don't approve of their theological or church background; we judge them by their neighborhood; we don't approve of their employment; we don't like their friends. Pharisees are masters at this. I remember that some people were surprised when I chose Jon Bush to be my first assistant at Westminster Chapel because he did not have a posh accent; he wasn't a Cockney, but he sounded a bit like one. (In Britain, much like America, a person's background is often detectable by their regional accent.)

People also criticized Arthur Blessitt when he wore jeans in our pulpit. I was criticized when I stopped wearing a Geneva gown. These are things that should not come into our minds—unless we want to be the Pharisees of our day.

It will be recalled that Pharisees strutted around in their garb because "everything they do is done for people to see," said Jesus (Matt. 23:5, NIV). This does not mean we are oblivious to the way we are seen in public. Of course not. I want to look nice. I make sure my hair is combed and that I have had a clean shave. But if I seek significance by my appearance or my clothes or whether or not I wear a suit or a tie, I have lapsed into a Pharisaical mode that is certainly not good.

Chances are you and I are Pharisees if:

13. We care more about people's opinions than God's.

Jesus said that the Jews were not able to believe in His Messiahship because they preferred the praise of one another rather than seeking God's praise. People ask, How could the Jews have missed their own Messiah? Here is the answer: they made no effort to seek the honor, glory, and praise of the Most High God. They chose the praise of each other. It is so sad. But we too could miss what God is doing in our day—and the direction He is taking—if we are controlled by the opinions of our peers, whether friends or enemies.

I've mentioned John 5:44 many times in this book, and that's because it is so integral to the concept of Pharisaism. The Greek word for *praise* in John 5:44 is *doxa,* which means glory, honor, or praise. It comes from a root word that means opinion.[3] This means that God has an opinion. We must make a choice: whose opinion matters? If we care more about what people think, we are Pharisees.

What is gravely serious is the very point I have made: by making no effort to obtain God's praise or opinion, they set themselves up for unbelief. But when the very Messiah they claimed they longed for came and was right under their noses, they did not recognize Him. All because they developed a habit of wanting the praise of people rather than of God.

This may seem a fairly innocuous tendency—since it is surely human to want people to compliment us. But making no effort to obtain His compliment and affirmation of them ended up cutting off their hope of seeing and enjoying God work in their own day.

Speaking personally, of all the points I am listing in this part of the book, this one is the premise I value most of all. I fear this more than anything else in the world: that I should want your approval of me more than God's.

I would define wisdom as *getting God's opinion*. The problem with so many of us is that we don't want His opinion. We are afraid that His opinion might militate against what we want for ourselves. And yet God's opinion will keep all of us out of trouble if we would get it and follow it.

The Greek *sophia*—wisdom—is available to all of us. The ancient Greeks thought that *sophia* was given only to the "gods"—Plato, Aristotle, Socrates. But the Bible promises wisdom to ordinary people like you and me—in two ways: (1) "the fear of the LORD is the beginning of wisdom" (Prov. 9:10, NIV); and (2) merely asking for it (Jas. 1:5).

It ought to be an assumption beyond debate that getting the wisdom of God is the greatest gift imaginable on this planet! Indeed, it is so valuable that we are urged to seek this above all else.

> Get wisdom. Though it cost all you have, get
> understanding. Cherish her, and she will exalt
> you; embrace her, and she will honor you. She
> will give you a garland to grace your head and
> present you with a glorious crown.
>
> —PROVERBS 4:7–9, NIV

It ultimately comes to this: esteeming God's praise
and honor above the praise of people. The consequence of not getting His praise is too great. I would
hate to think of what I may have missed over the years
merely because I cared more about what my friends
and enemies thought than what God thinks.

And yet this requires strength. You may stand alone.
But to be truly brave is the willingness to stand alone.
I often think of Paul's words in his final letter.

> At my first defense no one came to stand by me,
> but all deserted me.
>
> —2 TIMOTHY 4:16

Was it worth it, Paul? His reply: "There is laid up
for me the crown of righteousness, which the Lord,
the righteous judge, will award to me on that day"
(2 Tim. 4:8).

Chances are you and I are Pharisees if:

14. We need to be sure that people know about it if we give, pray, or fast.

You will recall that Jesus told us not to be like those who only gave, prayed, or fasted when such would be seen by people. Why was this so important? It is important because the principle we just looked at—that of John 5:44—is at stake. Jesus made it clear: if we do what we do to be seen of men, we get a reward, yes; but it is only in the here and now—the feeling that builds up our egos: the praise of people, not of God.

> Beware of practicing your righteousness before other people in order to be seen by them, for then you will have no reward from your Father who is in heaven. Thus when you give to the needy, sound no trumpet before you, as the hypocrites do in the synagogue and in the streets, that they may be praised by others. Truly I say to you, they have received their reward. But when you give to the needy, do not let your left hand know what your right hand is doing, so that your giving might be in secret. And your Father who sees in secret will reward you.
>
> —MATTHEW 6:1–4

The irony is, we actually develop a healthy ego, significance, and sense of self-esteem when we cultivate a habit of seeking only the praise of God. God has a way of doubling our sense of significance and self-worth.

He will not let us down. But when we choose to give, pray, or fast only when people are likely to find out, we risk repeating the fatal sin of the ancient Jews who utterly missed out on what God wanted them to receive. The same missing out can happen today as well.

I preached this principle throughout the whole of my ministry at Westminster Chapel. It would be fair to say that John 5:44 was the common denominator of all my preaching and teaching for twenty-five years. And yet I had to admit that not all got it!

For example, one of my most ardent supporters came into the vestry to see me shortly before he died to say he had designated a substantial sum of money in his will to Westminster Chapel. But this was with the understanding that a plaque in his honor be put up somewhere in the Chapel auditorium for people to see and therefore know what he had done. My heart sank. I couldn't believe it! Here was a man who stood by me and (I thought) appreciated my teaching thoroughly. And yet he put a request that suggested he had not learned a single thing from me! He wanted the praise of people after all—after he was gone. Oh dear! How our hearts are so eager to receive the praise of people.

A friend of mine purchased a large brick of clear glass with his name on it when the famous Crystal Cathedral—a reflective glass building in Garden

Grove, California—was being built many years ago. This was the way they raised money to build this amazing building. Hundreds of people bought these blocks of clear glass for $15,000 each with the promise that their names would be etched on each glass brick. One wonders if the building would have been erected had they not been motivated by the praise of people. It seats 2,248 people. The sad irony is that the building was sold a few years ago to the Catholic Diocese of Orange County that had no connection with the church's founder or people who made it happen.

Chances are you and I are Pharisees if:

15. We are motivated by money.

The Pharisees were "lovers of money" (Luke 16:14). This was partly why they ridiculed Jesus. So much of Jesus' teaching pertained to money. A case can be made that Jesus talked about money more than He did any other subject. It should not be surprising. For when all else is said about Pharisees, it follows that the love of money would be very close by. But, as we just saw above, what will make it easy for us to turn loose of our money is a promise of people finding out that we gave! This shows that pride runs almost parallel with our love of money.

Caution: the Bible does not say that money is a root of evil; Paul said that "the *love of* money is a root of all kinds of evils" (1 Tim. 6:10, emphasis added).

I referred above to one of the supporters of my

ministry who did not seem to grasp it fully, proving this when he asked for public recognition for his financial legacy to the Chapel. We had another family who loved my theology and teaching of the Law. They were such an encouragement. But this abruptly changed one day—over one sermon. My preaching and application of James 5:1–5 some forty years ago offended them. They shamelessly stopped coming to church and never came back. In this passage James condemns wealthy Christians who had abused poor Christians by withholding wages from them.

> Behold, the wages of the laborers who mowed your fields, which you kept back by fraud, are crying out against you, and the cries of the harvesters have reached the ears of the Lord of hosts. You have lived on the earth in luxury and in self-indulgence. You have fattened your hearts in a day of slaughter.
>
> —JAMES 5:4–5

I suspect that many of us have not taken seriously enough God's heart for poor people. You may recall my referring earlier to the fast in Isaiah 58—which also related to ancient Jews neglecting the poor. God has always been for the underdog. So often middle-class Christians glibly dismiss the plight of the poor and the homeless: "they are lazy" or "they should get a job," etc. It has been a fault of Christians from the days of the earliest church. They think they will get away with it.

The Corinthians thought this. In those days Christians met in homes—sometimes large homes—of wealthy Christians. What happened was this. They would have the Lord's Supper before the poorer Christians—who worked late—arrived. Consequently, the poor missed out on the Lord's Supper. Paul thundered: "It is not the Lord's supper that you eat" (1 Cor. 11:20). In other words, how dare you call it the Lord's Supper when the poor show up and are utterly left out of the fellowship? These well-to-do Christians thought that God had not noticed. Not only had He noticed but He stepped in to judge these Corinthian Christians. How?

> For anyone who eats and drinks without discerning the Lord's body eats and drinks judgment on himself. That is why many of you are weak and ill, and some have died.
> —1 Corinthians 11:29–30

God had judged them by afflicting them with ill health. Some were taken suddenly to heaven. Yes, it is what God did, says Paul. The proof that they were saved is that Paul says they were "judged by the Lord"—disciplined—rather than being "condemned along with the world" (1 Cor. 11:32)—which means going to hell.

But there is more we need to say regarding money. Is not the love of money at the bottom of many Christian ministries today? For example, the common denominator of the Charismatic Movement fifty years ago was the power and gifts of the Holy Spirit. But things have changed; today the common denominator without doubt is the "prosperity gospel." Paul said that the time would come that people would not endure sound teaching but would "accumulate for themselves teachers to suit their own passions, and will turn away from listening to the truth" (2 Tim. 4:3–4). Almost certainly it is the love of money that keeps some ministries alive—namely, the appeal to greed by saying, "Give to our ministry and God will prosper you." What is most lamentable is that this teaching has appealed largely to the poor—who have been some of the main ones to respond to such teaching. It is equally true that some of those who have thrived on prosperity teaching have changed their thinking about this.

Chances are you and I are Pharisees if:

16. We feel righteous by comparing ourselves to others.

Rather than measuring ourselves by the Word of God, we measure others. Instead of discovering the sinfulness of our own hearts, which is so painful, we immediately find someone nearby who we judge to be in bad shape and assume, by contrast, we are OK. But that is by comparison. Besides, we don't know what is in another's heart. Therefore when we get a righteous feeling by selecting someone we assume to be more wicked than ourselves, we totally avoid the very thing Jesus wants us to do; namely, to see what we are like before God and not in the eyes of people.

The tax collector, said Jesus in His parable, was justified because he felt so unworthy before God (Luke 18:13–14); the Pharisee was not justified because the only way he could feel good was to compare himself to the sinful tax collector. He felt better about himself but had no idea how he appeared before God. This is the very reason a Pharisee lacks objectivity about himself and is so superficial: he gets a smug feeling by finding someone he can look down on—and never give the matter another thought.

Sometimes people can feel they are highly spiritual and have God's approval—which can be entirely of the flesh—because they are successful. Such people can be judgmental, unreachable, and unteachable. I made a suggestion to a well-known preacher who had become very successful in a short period of time but who embraced preaching a prosperity gospel. He would not listen to me. His reason: "Why should I listen to you when you only preach to hundreds and I preach to thousands?" You can always tell a successful man, but you can't tell him much! The Laodiceans felt successful.

> For you say, I am rich, I have prospered, and I
> need nothing, not realizing you are wretched,
> pitiable, poor, blind, and naked. I counsel you
> to buy from me gold refined by fire, so that
> you may be rich, and white garments so that
> you may clothe yourself and the shame of your
> nakedness may not be seen, and salve to anoint
> your eyes, so that you may see.
>
> —REVELATION 3:17–18

Chances are you and I are Pharisees if:

Total Depravity

17. We have no sense of sin by our thoughts, only our deeds.

As I mentioned earlier, the Pharisees were offended by the teaching that what makes a person unclean is "what comes out of the mouth" rather than what goes in (Matt. 15:11–12). A good rule of thumb in assessing whether we are Pharisees is how we get a sense of sin. If it is only in what we do, then we can get off the hook quite a bit. We do not kill people. We do not steal. The Pharisees could only conceive of sin in terms of outward acts—as in most of the Ten Commandments. They seldom dwell on the tenth commandment, which has to do with the heart; mainly coveting, which is what convinced the righteous Saul of Tarsus that he really was a sinner after all (Rom. 7:7–9).

My own theological background did not prepare me for this most powerful and essential insight—that

153

sin is in our thoughts as in our deeds. You'll recall that what ultimately convinced me, apart from the conviction through the immediate and direct witness of the Spirit, were John's words, "If we claim to be without sin, we deceive ourselves and the truth is not in us" (1 John 1:8). Therefore, if we claim to be without sin merely because we have not done anything such as being sexually immoral, we are first self-deceived and second devoid of the truth.

The closer we get to God and the more honest we are with ourselves and our motives, the more we will find that Jeremiah got it right—that the heart is "deceitful above all things, and desperately sick." He added: "Who can understand it?" (Jer. 17:9).

Chances are you and I are Pharisees if:

18. We major on minors.

We do this a thousand ways of course, but the example Jesus gave when He said the Pharisees "strain out a gnat but swallow a camel" had to do with tithing (Matt. 23:23–24). A Pharisee is one who avoids personal obligation to the whole Law by keeping *some* of it; namely, rules which give them a good feeling that they are OK. Tithing does this nicely.

Now I believe in tithing, preach on this all over the world, and even wrote a book on it. Jesus also endorsed tithing when He said these things they "ought to have done" (v. 23). But there is a danger here. If someone tithes, they might tell themselves they are righteous because "most people don't." Moreover, the ancient Pharisees made sure they tithed by doing it across the board—tithing spices such as mint, dill, and cumin. Nothing is left out.

Never mind that there are weightier matters of the Law—like justice (caring for the poor), mercy (showing kindness to strangers), and faithfulness in thought and deed twenty-four hours a day. If we prove that we tithe, it counts for righteousness somehow (we tell ourselves).

I found it was sometimes easier to get Christians to tithe at Westminster Chapel than it was to get them out on the streets witnessing on a Saturday morning—or to totally forgive their enemies. It is like the rules in Jerusalem today. There are those who excuse all manner of sins, but they make sure they uphold dietary laws such as "Do not cook a young goat in its mother's milk" (Exod. 23:19, NIV). When brought forward to today, this means do not put mayonnaise on a beef sandwich! By being careful in this area, one thinks he or she is being holy.

Some of my fellow Christians in recent years have made a big deal over diet by trying to imagine what Jesus would eat. They assume that the Levitical Law must surely be safe to follow—that it was designed for our health. But my friend Rabbi Rosen assured me that health had nothing to do with the intent of the Law. In other words, the ancient Israelites were not allowed to eat pork or shellfish for reasons of holiness. But it has been assumed by some Christians it was because of health reasons.

Rabbi Rosen, an expert regarding this sort of thing, said emphatically to me, "The Levitical diet was all about holiness, not health." This means that orthodox Jews to this very day keep the letter of the dietary aspects of the Law entirely because they are to be different from the world—not because God was looking after their health. Yes, some may make a case that pork or lobster is not always good for you, but that is not why Jews were to avoid pork or lobster.

As for seafood that they *can* eat—as long as what lives in water has scales—they now have even found a way to eat the delicious mahi-mahi (used to be called dolphin in Florida), which obviously does not have scales. How do they manage this? By looking at these fish with a microscope, they convince themselves that they do have tiny scales! These fish truly are so tasty! I suppose catfish would come under the same category.

My point is this. Dietary laws in ancient Israel were not looking after our physical bodies or health but holiness. They were to be *different*. That was how they regarded holiness. Otherwise Jesus could not have pronounced all foods "clean" (Mark 7:19).

Whether by tithing or avoiding certain foods, some manage to feel they are more pleasing to God than others. By majoring on minors, some get a pious feeling.

Chances are you and I are Pharisees if:

19. We are experts in finding what might seem to be loopholes in the Bible to excuse certain areas of disobedience.

You'll recall that one of the loopholes of the ancient Pharisees was a way of avoiding responsibility to parents. Whereas the Law states, "Honor your father and your mother" (Exod. 20:12, NIV), the Pharisees said that money that should have been given to parents could be diverted to the synagogue (Matt. 15:5–6). Jesus said, "You break the command of God for the sake of your tradition" (Matt. 15:3). The Pharisees reasoned, "My parents don't need the money, but the synagogue does."

We can do that today in many ways. For example, my church (the storehouse) doesn't need the money; I need to pay my bills, which God would want me to do. We create our own loopholes. I did this years ago—when Louise and I were first married. I reasoned that God would want me to pay my bills first, then start tithing. A year later I was even deeper in debt. Two years later I was even worse off! But mercifully one day we began tithing—though still in debt. We were debt-free in two years, and I have been out of debt for almost sixty years.

Another example: We excuse ourselves from

forgiving others because they are not sorry. Or they have not apologized. Or they need to repent first. I get a letter once a year from the same man who rejects my teaching of total forgiveness—but has come up with a reason. In a word: he says that God does not forgive us unless we repent first; therefore, we don't have to forgive people until they repent.

My reply: God forgave us at the cross while we were still sinners—"while we were still weak," Christ died for the "ungodly" (Rom. 5:6, 8). Jesus did not condemn the woman found in adultery but said, "Neither do I condemn you, and from now on sin no more" (John 8:11).

At the cross there was nobody sorry for what they did to Jesus—neither the soldiers nor the priests—and yet Jesus said, "Father, forgive them, for they do not know what they are doing" (Luke 23:34, NIV). Our model is to be Jesus, not the Pharisees.

Warning to all: if you are looking for a loophole to avoid forgiving hardened and unrepentant enemies, you have come up with a recipe for staying bitter forever. It is easy to forgive when people are sorry; it is extremely hard to forgive when they are not sorry. My suggestion again: get a major victory by forgiving them when they are not the slightest bit sorry or aware of their hurting us. Otherwise, I lovingly say to you if that is your rationale, you almost certainly will go to your grave a loser and an extremely sad person. I plead with you: totally forgive them, and you will be released.

Chances are you and I are Pharisees if:

20. We are more concerned to uphold our theology than to help people.

We saw earlier how the Pharisees could not bring themselves to rejoice that a blind man was healed because the healing took place on the Sabbath. It is good when we hold sound theology high in our priorities. I call myself a theologian, and I love theology. But there comes a time when I must accept that God will use a person who is not in agreement with my thinking. When God uses a person whose theology I could pick to pieces, which is more important? To scold him for his error or to rejoice that God uses such a person to see people blessed, healed, and delivered?

To not rejoice in someone being blessed, no matter the instrument God uses, merely because I don't agree with the person makes me a Pharisee. God may use one whose theology is different, whose church is different, and whose culture is different. I should affirm what God does through a person I may not particularly like. Or agree with.

One of my solemn awakenings over the years was having to admit God uses surprising people to do His work. I should have learned this lesson many years ago. I came across a man whose first name was Garland in Fort Lauderdale who was running a rescue mission.

I was told about him by my old friend Jesse Oakley, who had a severe back problem. Jesse could hardly walk and was in extreme pain. Garland put his hand on Jesse's back. Jesse was healed on the spot and came home walking without pain. I wanted to meet Garland. But there was a problem: Garland had a "Jesus only" theology. He was also uneducated.

Still uncertain of him, I invited him to our home for dinner. I debated in my mind all evening whether to tell him about a severe problem Louise had: she could not open her mouth wide; it hurt if she opened it more than an inch. She had trouble eating. She had this problem for a good while. Just as Garland was leaving, I decided to ask him to pray for her. He put his briefcase down and put his hand on her jaw and said, "Be healed in Jesus' name." She quickly opened her mouth wide—something she had not been able to do in months. He picked up his briefcase and casually walked to his car as if this happens in his ministry all the time! Louise's problem never returned.

I should not have been so surprised. Then or now. After all, I have often quoted Romans 9:15, NIV, in my preaching, "I will have mercy on whom I have mercy." God even shows mercy on those who don't have sound theology like me! God's ways are higher than our ways and His thoughts higher than our thoughts (Isa. 55:9).

Chances are you and I are Pharisees if:

21. We love to score theological points with our enemies.

Two of the ancient parties in Judaism were the Pharisees (in some ways the fundamentalists of their day) and the Sadducees (in some ways the liberals of their day). They had in common a hatred for Jesus. But each still got their thrills by making their rivals look bad. When the Pharisees noted gleefully that Jesus had silenced the Sadducees with His argument against them regarding resurrection (Matt. 23:34), they immediately wanted to have their turn at challenging Jesus. In other words, while applauding Jesus, both Pharisees and Sadducees took shots at each other; this sort of thing got them worked up and excited.

The apostle Paul knew this and played into the rivalry brilliantly when he was being tried. He said before the Sanhedrin that he was on trial because of his hope in the resurrection of the dead. "When he said this, a dispute broke out between the Pharisees and the Sadducees, and the assembly was divided." The episode got Paul out of a difficult situation and bought him more time (Acts 23:6–10).

I am reminded of two churches (reportedly in Alabama), one a Methodist (which practiced infant baptism and believed you could lose your salvation if you sinned), the other Baptist (who practiced baptism by immersion and believed you could never lose your salvation). The two churches ran missions concurrently, but the Baptists were heard later to say, "Well, we didn't have much of a revival, but thank God the Methodists didn't either." Vintage Pharisaism.

Chances are you and I are Pharisees if:

22. We claim God's approval of us rather than our rivals because we "know" our theology, not theirs, is sound.

The party spirit that emerged from the rivalry between Sadducees and Pharisees kept them apart and fueled their motivation to score points. But at bottom the Pharisees knew that God must be with them rather than their opponents because of such teachings as the resurrected life beyond the grave and belief in angels. The Sadducees did not believe in these (Acts 23:8), and the Pharisees knew these truths were solidly based in their Law and traditions; therefore, God would decidedly be on their side. This gave them a superior feeling.

They did not think—they *knew*—that they were on the side of the angels. It did not bother them at all that right before their eyes was God's very Son, whom they did not recognize. It is so easy for us to take ourselves so seriously because we assume that God would be on the side of the party who is "sounder." Really? He may well feel toward us as Jesus did the Pharisees.

Earlier I referred to Romans 9:15, arguably the most powerful verse in the Bible to demonstrate the sovereignty of God. I can never forget that on the day of my first major experience of the Holy Spirit—October 31, 1955, when I saw the face of Jesus—I also experienced firsthand what I would call an embryonic understanding of predestination.

I had never read a word of a Calvinist in my life (except for Jonathan Edwards' sermon "Sinners in the Hands of Angry God"). But before that day was over, my theology changed forever. Days later I read Romans 9:15, and that made me see truth I would have never thought I would believe. I was brought up both Arminian (free will teaching with the belief you could lose your salvation) and Wesleyan (the teaching of Christian perfection, which influenced me for good and ill).

I quoted Romans 9:15 to Dr. William Greathouse, Dean of Religion at Trevecca at that time. (He later became president of Trevecca and a general superintendent of the Church of the Nazarene.) He said, "R. T., you are going off into Calvinism."

I said, "What is that?"

He said, "We don't believe that."

I replied, "Then we are wrong." And I added, "Will you tell me what Romans 9:15 means?"

He said, "Give me a little time to think about that." Who would have thought that sixty years later Trevecca would give me a Doctor of Divinity degree (owing to Dr. Greathouse's influence)?

As Paul said, "Oh, the depth of the riches and

wisdom and knowledge of God! How unsearchable are his judgments and how inscrutable his ways!" (Rom. 11:33). It was Romans 11:33 that Dr. Martyn Lloyd-Jones quoted to me when referring to the fact that I became a successor to him at Westminster Chapel.

And what does Romans 9:15 mean? I answer: God, being God, has the sovereign right to do what He wills with whomever He chooses. In Romans 9:15 Paul was actually quoting Exodus 33:19, NIV: "I will have mercy on whom I have mercy, and I will have compassion on whom I have compassion." According to Paul we were chosen "not because of our works" but rather according to God's own "purpose and grace" (2 Tim. 1:9).

Jesus claimed that "all" that were given to Him by the Father "will come to me, and whoever comes to me I will never cast out" (John 6:37). He added, "No one can come to me unless the Father who sent me draws him" (John 6:44).

As Luke observed when referring to salvation being given to the Gentiles, "As many as were appointed to eternal life believed" (Acts 13:48). Some think that Luke should have said that "as many as believed were appointed to eternal life." But he was intentionally making a theological statement. I discussed this with my Greek teacher at Southern Baptist Theological Seminary. He admitted that Luke actually said, "as many as were appointed [ordained] to eternal life believed," but added (sadly): "I disagree with Luke." Oh dear.

Likewise, God can choose the instruments of His choice to bless and also to heal! We are wrong to suppose that God will not manifest His power through them until they get sorted out theologically! What if God waits until we all get to heaven before we get full correction of our doctrine—but uses us sovereignly in the meantime?

That said, I suspect God might, in some cases, withhold His blessing from us if we ignore good teaching when it is available. He *is* a God of truth and may choose to manifest His glory by *correcting* us when the honor of His name is at stake. But do *any* of us have perfect understanding of God's ways? No. Being glorified (Rom. 8:30; 1 John 3:3) will include not only the transformation of our mortal bodies but transformation of our inadequate minds. That way nobody will be able to point the finger gleefully at their theological opponent—in heaven or even on earth (should God choose to show His glory now). We all have so much to learn. But the Pharisee doesn't think so.

One of my most humbling moments was having to admit that the Revival we prayed for at Westminster Chapel passed us by. I was so sure it would come to us. I felt we had surely borne the heat of the day. We had our days of prayer and fasting. We had taken to the streets. I had put my ministry and reputation on the line. We had prayed for the manifestation of God's glory in our midst, but God chose to manifest

His glory by passing us by! After all, He is sovereign; He can have mercy on whom He will! Not that we did not have a touch of His blessing when *and* after Arthur Blessitt came to us. And we saw people converted and delivered from the demonic and saw people unquestionably healed, including a Muslim lady who had throat cancer (which led to her conversion). But what we prayed and hoped for never came.

Many living today can verify how I used to say publicly when at Westminster Chapel, "What if revival came to All Souls and Langham Place, but not to us? Would we affirm it? What if revival came to Kensington Temple but not to us, would we affirm it?" Mind you, to be transparently truthful, I never for a moment thought I would have to do something like that—I was *so* sure that glorious revival would come to us! But it didn't. And when I heard that the Spirit of God was unusually at work at Holy Trinity Brompton, I had serious problems. I felt betrayed. Surely God would not do that in an Anglican church (we all know that the Church of England is apostate!). He surely would not bless those Etonians with their upper-class posh accents!

But He did.

I was completely wrong!

Chances are you and I are Pharisees if:

23. We easily dismiss a person we don't like or disagree with because we are able to find something truly wrong with them.

This is an old Pharisaical tactic: to find something you know is undoubtedly wrong; therefore, you are at utter peace in rejecting that person entirely. The Pharisees found what they had been looking for: Jesus claimed to be able to forgive sins. What? Forgive sins? Blasphemy! Who can forgive sins but God alone? Jesus calmly asked, "Which is easier, to say, 'Your sins are forgiven you' or to say, 'Rise and walk'?" (Luke 5:21–23).

We do this too. When we hope we don't have to accept someone, we look for something we know is absolutely wrong in them; therefore, we have the excuse we need not to affirm them. "He baptizes by sprinkling." "This man baptizes by immersion." "He speaks in tongues." "She has not been baptized in the Holy Spirit."

You may recall the Pharisee who invited Jesus to have dinner with him. A "woman of the city who was a sinner" wiped Jesus' feet with her tears. The Pharisee was testing Jesus. The Pharisee said to himself that if Jesus were truly a prophet He would discern what kind of woman this was (Luke 7:37–39). The Pharisee looked for a reason not to believe in Jesus. Of course, Jesus knew and gave the Pharisee—named Simon—one of His parables (Luke 7:40–50).

When we find what we are looking for, namely, a

glaring fault or theological difference with them, we tell ourselves, "Don't worry about not affirming this person—we know what is seriously wrong with him (or her)." I knew a Baptist preacher in Fort Lauderdale (now in heaven) who spoke against the late Dr. D. James Kennedy, senior minister of Coral Ridge Presbyterian Church of Fort Lauderdale. The latter church was the fastest growing church of Fort Lauderdale if not all of America at the time. Dr. Kennedy was busy winning souls through his program called Evangelism Explosion while this poor Baptist preacher (whose church was less than a mile away from Coral Ridge) could not recognize his own jealousy. But he claimed that the only reason he was opposed to Dr. Kennedy was that Jim Kennedy was not a premillennialist but an amillennialist; Jim did not believe in a literal one-thousand-year reign of Jesus on earth after the second coming.

Even Pontius Pilate could see that it was jealousy that lay behind the Jews wanting to have Jesus crucified (Mark 15:10). We can always detect jealousy in others; we hate to admit that jealousy is what lies behind so many of our own motives.

Chances are you and I are Pharisees if:

24. We say, "We are more in tune with God than you are."

The thing above all else that motivated the Pharisees and justified their existence in their own eyes was this: they thought they were more righteous than anybody else because of their good works. As Luke puts it, they "trusted in themselves that they were righteous." They could actually say to God, "I thank you that I am not like other men," and reminded God of their righteous deeds. They also "treated others with contempt" (Luke 18:9–12).

This principle may apply to us in many ways, but hopefully not because one reading these lines is trusting in his or her righteousness. However, let me mention two ways that should give us pause if we are caring about others. This may apply to Word people and Spirit people. So many of us who embrace the gifts of the Holy Spirit, I fear, give the impression that we think we are more spiritual than others. Some of us seem to think, "If you don't speak in tongues, you are not as spiritual as I am," or, "If you haven't experienced the gifts of the Spirit, you are not really in touch with God." Such people make some Evangelical Christians feel second-class, and this attitude, which I can only call Pharisaical, helps erect a wall that divides Christians from Christians.

Never forget that King Saul *on his way to kill young David* demonstrated that his gift of prophecy was in good working order. Difficult though this is to understand—in fact I don't understand it—"the Spirit of God came upon him," and he prophesied so amazingly that it was said, "Is Saul also among the prophets?" (1 Sam. 19:23–24). Figure that out! My only explanation:

it is because the gifts and calling of God are "irrevocable" (Rom. 11:29—"without repentance," KJV). This verse means that a gift of the Spirit comes to you not because you have repented more deeply than others and also that it stays with you whether or not your ways are pleasing to Him. This means that you should never—ever—imagine that you are a cut above other Christians because you have a prophetic gift or you speak or pray in tongues.

But a word to Word people is needed here. So many of them (including me) certainly give this impression, that we are more on God's wavelength than other Christians. "If you don't believe in the sovereignty of God as we do, you are not a faithful believer." Or, "If you don't believe in predestination and the eternal security of the believer, you don't really know the God of the Bible." I even heard a preacher from New Orleans say: "If you don't believe these doctrines, you are not saved." Such a spirit, which I can only call Pharisaical, alienates many other Christians and makes them feel they are theologically illiterate.

Chances are you and I are Pharisees if:

25. We call another person a "Pharisee."

If I call you a Pharisee, I am a Pharisee. When I say, "The trouble with you is that you are always judging people," I just judged you. When I point the finger at you for pointing the finger, I too point the finger. "Do not judge, or you too will be judged" (Matt. 7:1, NIV).

What does one do? Answer: we must learn to control the tongue. "God is in heaven and you are on earth so let your words be few" (Eccles. 5:2, NIV). When words are many, transgression is not lacking, but whoever restrains his lips is prudent" (Prov. 10:19).

The truth is, the Pharisee lurks in all of us. This means we would be among those Jesus condemned the most. This fact alone ought to catapult us out of our comfort zone and make us see not only our self-righteousness but also how grateful we should be that God saved us. We don't deserve to be saved. God was simply kind. Good. Merciful. He saved Saul of Tarsus, the Pharisee of the Pharisees indeed. And Saul, called Paul, never got over it. He thanked God as best he could as long as he lived.

If God could save Paul, He could save anybody. If God could save you, He could save anybody. If God could save me, He could save anybody. Why did He do it? I don't know and probably will never know. I can only spend the rest of my life doing my best to thank Him and show Him how thankful I am.

May God the Father, God the Son, and God the Holy Spirit be with you and abide with you now and evermore. Amen.

Notes

Introduction

1. "G. K. Chesterton Quotes," Goodreads, accessed May 14, 2020, https://www.goodreads.com/quotes/472033-it-is-the-test-of-a-good-religion-whether-you.

Chapter 1

1. The Free Dictionary, s.v. "pharisaism," accessed September 10, 2020, https://www.thefreedictionary.com/pharisaism.

Chapter 2

1. John Newton, "In Evil I Took Delight," Hymnary.org, accessed May 12, 2020, https://hymnary.org/hymn/H4AC1869/L41.

2. "Obesity Consequences," Harvard T. H. Chan School of Public Health, accessed February 18,

2020, https://www.hsph.harvard.edu/obesity-prevention-source/obesity-consequences/.

Chapter 3

1. Bible Hub, s.v. "*besta*," accessed February 18, 2020, https://biblehub.com/isaiah/57-17.htm.
2. Blue Letter Bible, s.v. "*philargyros*," accessed February 18, 2020, https://www.blueletterbible.org/lang/lexicon/lexicon.cfm?Strongs=G5366&t=KJV.

Chapter 4

1. Robert Robinson, "Come, Thou Fount of Every Blessing," Hymnary.org, accessed May 13, 2020, https://hymnary.org/text/come_thou_fount_of_every_blessing.
2. Robert Robinson, "Come, Thou Fount of Every Blessing," The Nazarene Hymnal, accessed May 13, 2020, https://hymnary.org/hymn/PWNH1951/56.
3. R. T. Kendall, *The Sermon on the Mount*, (Bloomington, MN: Chosen Books, 2011), https://www.amazon.com/

Sermon-Mount-R-T-Kendall-ebook/dp/
B005OYUHCI#reader_B005OYUHCI.

Chapter 6

1. As quoted in Jill Briscoe, *Running on Empty* (Fort Washington, PA: CLC Publications, 1988).
2. Graham Kendrick, "Restore, O Lord," Make Way Music, accessed May 15, 2020, https://www.grahamkendrick.co.uk/songs/graham-kendrick-songs/the-king-is-among-us/restore-o-lord.
3. Blue Letter Bible, s.v. "*doxa*," accessed February 18, 2020, https://www.blueletterbible.org/lang/lexicon/lexicon.cfm?Strongs=G1391&t=KJV.